AMERICAN

HERITAGE

October 1959 · Volume X, Number 6

This fanciful water color, which combines patriotic sentiment with a bucolic view of the arrival of the Great Navigator in 1492, was painted around 1825 by an unknown artist. It belongs to the New York State Historical Association in Cooperstown. The well-dressed red men are ready for peace or war. Little do they know.

AMERICAN HERITAGE

The Magazine of History

PUBLISHER
James Parton
EDITORIAL DIRECTOR
Joseph J. Thorndike, Jr.

EDITOR
Bruce Catton
MANAGING EDITOR
Oliver Jensen
EXECUTIVE EDITOR
Eric Larrabee
ASSOCIATE EDITORS
Richard M. Ketchum
Joan Paterson Mills
ASSISTANT EDITOR
Robert L. Reynolds
EDITORIAL ASSISTANTS
Caroline Backlund, Helen M. Brown
Robert Cowley, Stephen W. Sears
COPY EDITOR
Beverly Hill
ASSISTANT: Naomi S. Weber

ART DIRECTOR
Irwin Glusker
ASSOCIATE ART DIRECTOR: Murray Belsky
STAFF PHOTOGRAPHER: Herbert Loebel

ADVISORY BOARD
Allan Nevins, *Chairman*
Ray A. Billington   Louis C. Jones
Carl Carmer   Richard P. McCormick
Albert B. Corey   Harry Shaw Newman
Christopher Crittenden Howard H. Peckham
Marshall B. Davidson   S. K. Stevens
Arthur M. Schlesinger, Sr.

CIRCULATION DIRECTOR
Richard V. Benson

AMERICAN HERITAGE is published every two months by American Heritage Publishing Co., Inc., 551 Fifth Avenue, New York 17, N. Y.
Single Copies: $2.95
Annual Subscriptions: $12.50 in U.S. & Canada
$13.50 elsewhere

An annual Index of AMERICAN HERITAGE is published every February, priced at $1.00. AMERICAN HERITAGE is also indexed in *Readers' Guide to Periodical Literature.*

AMERICAN HERITAGE will consider but assumes no responsibility for unsolicited material.

Second class postage paid at New York, N. Y.

Sponsored by

American Association for State & Local History · Society of American Historians

CONTENTS   *October 1959 · Volume X, Number 6*

THE WAR TO END WAR *by Laurence Stallings* 4

THE HERALD ANGELS OF WOMAN'S RIGHTS *by Peter Lyon* . . 18

FRANCISCO THE INCREDIBLE *by Fred J. Cook* 22

NEW YORK FERRY BOATS 26

AMERICAN HERITAGE BOOK SELECTION
EDISON: LAST DAYS OF THE WIZARD *by Matthew Josephson* . 32

TIMID PRESIDENT? FUTILE WAR? *by Irving Brant* . . . 46

PILGRIMS AND PURITANS *by A. L. Rowse* 48
(THE ELIZABETHANS AND AMERICA: PART IV)

THE ULTIMATE COURAGE OF JEAN DE BREBEUF
by Robert L. Reynolds 54

"I HAVE SUPPED FULL ON HORRORS" *from Fanny Seward's diary; edited and with an introduction by Patricia Carley Johnson* . . 60

THE *CARONDELET* RUNS THE GANTLET *by Phillips Melville* . 66

READING, WRITING, AND HISTORY *by Eric Larrabee* . . 73

A MORAL IN THE MAIL: *Envelopes from the Civil War* . . . 90

A SLAVE'S MEMORY OF MR. JEFFERSON 112

COVER: Behind wooden drums like this, which once beat for the Ninth Regiment, Vermont Volunteers, U.S. Infantry, thousands upon thousands of men and boys marched to war in answer to Lincoln's call. Mere youngsters carried the drums themselves, setting time to music, signaling retreat and charge, and, as the pipers do for Scotsmen, stiffening men's backs when they needed it most in battle. Save for parades, the drums are relatively still in modern war—there were none at Tarawa, or Anzio, or Hiroshima—but they nonetheless played as the young men sailed to France in World War I. In this issue a man who knew it well, Laurence Stallings, writes movingly of the spirit of those times, in "The War to End War." Our drum belongs to the Chicago Historical Society and is reproduced from a rendering lent by the Index of American Design at the National Gallery of Art, Washington, D.C. *Back Cover:* This World War I recruiting poster, by Howard Chandler Christy, is from the U.S. Navy; its appeal to young men and boys, like the drum's, is very ancient too.

It was an innocent man's war, a simple matter for Americans, despite the millions of Europeans who lay dead already between Vilna and the Marne. We entered the tragedy at the beginning of the fifth act, like off-stage soldiers in a play; and we entered singing. Woodrow Wilson had given us our simple theme: Kaiser Bill was a villain; and we marched to make the world safe for democracy.

Our weapons were simply modifications of earlier ones. Substitute the flimsy aircraft of the day with their remarkable pilots for the balloonist-professors of the Civil War, and General Pershing could have used Lee or Grant as a corps commander after routine briefing. We had the bolt-action rifle, and a bayonet that is still unchanged. Then there were machine guns, a medley of them. There were some grenades and mortars and, for artillery, the French gave us the seventy-five, which our own crews, in true American fashion, subjected to a cadence of firing that both astonished and alarmed the French. They supplied us with tanks, too; and for a large part of our two big pushes, crewed them for us. But for his set pattern of tactics, General Pershing took to open warfare.

We had begun with some exercises in trench warfare along quiet sectors; but Pershing, in his first full-dress conference with Generalissimo Foch, announced his intention of reducing the formidable German salient at Saint-Mihiel, an engineering masterpiece that had repulsed both British and French for four years. And he would take the salient with doughboys in tin hats and rolled leggings, all moving forward in frontiersman style, whether they

Charles Meurer depicted the World War I field kit of a U.S. Army officer—complete with spurs, a lighted cigarette, and the canteen that was still standard issue a quarter century later—in a trompe l'oeil *painting called* Memories.

THE WAR TO END WAR

We went into it singing, and forty years—which included a second world war—have not dimmed its terrible gallantry

By LAURENCE STALLINGS

were farm boys from Iowa or pushcart lads from Manhattan.

It was largely, at the outset, a singing war devoted to polite songs. There were croaks about K-K-K-Katy, Beautiful Katy, who would find a man waiting beside the k-k-k-kitchen door. Then some sang that it was a long way to Berlin, "but we'll get there, Uncle Sam will find a way." There was some anticipation of the joys awaiting a man on leave: "How you Gonna Keep 'em Down on the Farm, after They've Seen Paree?" Then there was a great marching song, "Over There," which the lads overseas changed to "Underwear," with some unprintable allusions to the long drawers furnished by the quartermaster's department. But the song of songs was "Mademoiselle from Armentières," and many a platoon waited for the wit of the team to fashion new versions of that young lady's extraordinary versatility and prowess. I recall that, as a young lieutenant, my first platoon had a whole series of verses on the Mademoiselle describing the nine months of gestation in great physiological detail, terminating with the arrival in the world of a little marine. They sang these verses with great good will until one afternoon we marched to its cadences past a garden wall, unaware of the fact that our battalion commander was giving a tea party to some ladies of the *haute noblesse* behind it.

General Pershing made his declaration as to the Saint-Mihiel salient in September, 1917. He was exactly one year in preparing for the day when his men, a new army green in many divisions, would go forward with rifle and bayonet and fulfill his mission. In the winter of 1918 we had some troops manning trenches in quiet sectors while General Pershing steadfastly refused to piecemeal his troops, battalion by battalion, into British and French units. It is a tribute to his character that he could withstand the entreaties of men like Lloyd George and Clemenceau, formidable antagonists. A casual raid or two by the Germans, catching some of us napping, meanwhile set about a wagging of heads in London and Paris, with the happiest of smiles in Berlin. Then the First Division staged its *divertissement* at Cantigny, and the real American war was on.

The Germans sustained their first true shock on the Marne around Château-Thierry, where Pershing threw in whole divisions for the first time, to bolster a shattered French line; but it was not his kind of a war. It was largely defensive, with occasional passages to the offensive, as witness the flamboyant charges of the Marine Brigade in Belleau Wood. It was the first true lesson for us, and the Germans administered it with great severity. I recall leading a digging party back from the vicinity of a town called Torcy, and watching a German sausage balloon ascending into the dawn sky. I took to the woods, hearing myself cursed by men swarming through brambles to follow. They were silent when we skirted a sunken road, for the soldiers there, grotesque in their attitudes of death, were still warm from a salvo directed by that balloon. We were new, we were ignorant, all of us; it was a matter of degree, but not of kind. And the Germans were teaching us.

No longer would the British and French ask for battalions to be brigaded into their war-weary troops. They would ask for divisions. In the July and August that followed, the requests were continuous, and battle streamers fly from many of our flags with the names of actions only the men who fought them will remember. Who recalls Foch's great counterattack at Soissons? The bloody gallantry at Mont Blanc? The Ourcq River, a little stream where a poet named Joyce Kilmer died? Pershing would lend these divisions, and by September recover enough of them to command an army of half a million men, his own men, with many of his divisions now battle-worthy.

The temper of the singing men with the wooden guns was changing. Hospitals were filling with too many their buddies would not forget—and there were no "miracle" drugs in that war. There must have been little difference between the hospital where Oliver Wendell Holmes found his son after Antietam, and a tent I recall somewhere near the vicinity of La-Ferte-Sous-Jarre. It was mainly a gangrene tent, where some of us suffered from that torment. In those days the commander of our brigade's machine-gun battalion sat bolt upright, quietly smoking away his agony. A lieutenant I had trained with would emerge from his delirium to apologize for the noise he knew he must have been making. There was no sulfa, no

penicillin, to still the air. There was only morphine sulfate, and those who survived that tent had a steep cliff to climb before they could rid themselves of morphine's toxic baggage.

The first glimpse of German prisoners, those fellows Woodrow Wilson told us we were not making war against, was always a pleasant experience for green troops. Yanks stood by, hacking open tins of bully beef to see other men, trembling in *Feldgrau*, devour food scorned by the lads from Des Moines and Seattle. As the hospitals filled, as new divisions suffered from the accomplished deviltry of the veteran Germans, this attitude would change. Moreover, there was one provocation unknown in the Second World War. It was poison gas. It was everywhere. Gas had been introduced in secrecy by the Germans, but they failed to win a war by its surprise use. Time went on, and both sides possessed it. Many a platoon leader would strip down his men to find them lobster-pink at armpit and groin, eyes swollen half-shut, breath hard-caught.

Meanwhile Saint-Mihiel's salient, a thorn in the Allied breast, was reduced by an American army with an element of surprise and a great *élan* in the attack. The first trial of true strength had been won; the great trial, the Argonne, lay ahead. Had it been left to Pershing, the name of Argonne would never have flown from a regimental staff. He had wished to push on from his victory at Saint-Mihiel, but the British protested to Foch. They had known a great day themselves on August 8 at Amiens, "the black day," Ludendorff said, "of the German army in the history of the war." The British under Haig wanted Pershing to reduce pressure on their right flank. They had begun asking for battalions, and progressed to requests for divisions, and now they wanted armies. Specifically, they wanted Pershing, who now commanded two American armies, to recapture the Argonne forest where for four years the Germans, who possess great skill in the use of fortifications, had been busy with their engineers devising tunnels and traps calculated to discourage the most aggressive opponent. Pershing, for once tractable, agreed to take the Argonne.

The saga of the Argonne is epitomized in the story of the Lost Battalion, those tough unfortunates from a New York division whose battalion commander had pushed forward into a trap. My own thoughts of it are colored by the memory of a wounded lieutenant from that outfit who was placed in a bed next to mine. He had lain for some days on the raw earth of the Argonne with multiple wounds and little care. His broken jaws were wired, front teeth extracted so he might sip nourishment through a tube. Both arms were

TEXT CONTINUED ON PAGE 84
A PORTFOLIO OF AMERICAN WAR PAINTINGS BEGINS ON THE PAGE OPPOSITE

A WAR PORTFOLIO BY AMERICAN ARTISTS

For a World War I America, Harvey Dunn's steel-helmeted and khaki-clad machine gunner (above) was the heroic prototype of the conscript warrior; just as Kerr Eby's painting of massed infantry marching to the front in the Saint-Mihiel offensive of September, 1918, (below) symbolized a conflict that for private soldier and general alike became somber and incomprehensible.

7

THE NAVY
NEEDS YOU!
DON'T READ
AMERICAN HISTORY—
MAKE IT!

U·S·NAVY RECRUITING STATION
34 E. 23rd St., N.Y. & 23 N. Broadway, Yonkers, N.Y.

THE WAR
OF THE POSTERS

Not the least of World War I's innovations was the systematic use of mass propaganda. Posters like those on this page, drawn by artists who probably got no closer to the war than a New York drawing board, may seem mawkish today but were surprisingly effective in arousing bellicose enthusiasm in a nation that had first regarded the European conflict with nervous indifference. Some resorted to catchy slogans (upper left); some conjured up the image of the barbaric Hun (bottom left); others were pitched for the ladies of the home front who canned sauerkraut and called it "liberty cabbage." A more direct appeal was James Montgomery Flagg's Uncle Sam (opposite), which stood the test of time so well that it was used again in the Second World War.

REMEMBER
·BELGIUM·

Buy Bonds
Fourth
Liberty
Loan

CAN
Vegetables
Fruit AND
the Kaiser too

Tomatoes
Peas
Monarch Brand
Unsweetened

Write for Free Book to
National War Garden Commission
WASHINGTON, D.C.

Charles Lathrop Pack—President   P. S. Ridsdale—Secretary

I WANT YOU
FOR U.S. ARMY
NEAREST RECRUITING STATION

"LAFAYETTE,
WE ARE HERE!"

America's mobilization, once under way, was rapid. In spite of the ever-present U-boat menace, fast convoys like the one shown in Burnell Poole's painting (above) ferried more than 2,000,000 men to France by November, 1918. Pushed in four years to the limits of their endurance, the Allies welcomed the Americans as their deliverers. The frenzied exchange between doughboys leaving for the front and the citizens of a Paris suburb (upper right) was a scene often repeated in the last year of the war. Gradually the Americans took their place in the trench system that stretched from the North Sea to Switzerland; like Dunn's sentry (right), with grenades and can-shaped Mills bombs close by, the newcomers stared uneasily across no man's land, and prepared for their first taste of a brutal, molelike warfare in which the capture of a few dozen yards was reckoned as a smashing victory.

10

A GALLERY OF

Two Congressional Medal of Honor winners were painted by Joseph Cummings Chase. Sergeant Alvin York (far left) wiped out a battalion of 35 machine guns singlehanded; Samuel Woodfill (left), whom General Pershing called "the outstanding soldier in the A.E.F.," was cited for a similar feat in the Argonne.

A.E.F. artist Dunn sketched German prisoners and American wounded streaming back from the front lines during the Meu

FIGHTING MEN

Chase also painted Douglas MacArthur (right) and General John J. ("Black Jack") Pershing (far right). Decorated for his courage in action, and twice wounded, MacArthur was a division commander at thirty-eight. Pershing, as leader of the American Expeditionary Forces, refused to scatter it among the other Allied troops.

...rgonne offensive of October, 1918. In these gaunt faces reflecting war's horror, it is difficult to tell victor from vanquished.

The Sniper, by Harvey Dunn

The Boche Looter, *by Harvey Dunn*

Above: Standing over the body of a fallen comrade, a dough-boy fires at the enemy in Dunn's sketch of street combat.

A Château-Thierry street barricade (below) was painted by W. J. Aylward. Here we won our first major engagement.

"AND WE WON'T COME BACK TILL IT'S OVER OVER THERE"

From the first reckless encounters at Château-Thierry in June, 1918, through the last dreadful days of the Meuse-Argonne offensive, when the German line finally cracked, the Americans acquitted themselves brilliantly; but the 48,000 killed in battle that they left behind testified to the high price of their courage. The scene at left, painted by W. J. Aylward, was typical of many such farewells on the battlefields of France. Back home the nation waited jubilantly for the boys to return. The march of the visiting French Blue Devils down Fifth Avenue in May, 1918 (above), painted by George Luks, set the tone for the gaudy American victory parades still to come.

This enthusiastic feminist sounded the Suffrage Call for a 1912 parade.

CULVER SERVICE

For half a century Susan Anthony

and Elizabeth Stanton lifted their

trumpets, and the echoes still resound

By PETER LYON

On a mild May morning in 1851, in the pleasant Finger Lakes town of Seneca Falls in central New York, two young women—genteel females, in the phrase then current—met on a street corner, were introduced, nodded affably, smiled, and went each on her way. It was a momentous encounter. In irrelevant ways the two females differed: one was matron, the other maiden; one was plump and soft, the other lean and bony; one was merry, the other grave, even grim at times. But on the essential point they were so like as to be one: each was a born reformer, and each, as she looked about her, saw much to reform. The matron was Mrs. Elizabeth Cady Stanton, the maiden was Miss Susan B. Anthony; and the two made a team that was destined, in the next half-century, to shake the orthodox of both sexes by the scruff of their customs until their faith rattled.

Back to this first brief meeting have been traced such portents of national doom as the emergence of Mom and Momism, the decline of the American male, the growth of the servant problem, the appearance of the ranch-type house, the decay of the double standard, the rise in cigarette smoking, and the marked sag of morals generally. Viewed through other, rosier spectacles, Mrs. Stanton and Miss Anthony were heroines of immense water who conjointly freed their sisters from male bondage, thereby enabling them to vote, get divorced, wear sensible clothes, own their own property, and even occasionally go Dutch treat with their male escorts. All of these phenomena, fair or foul, real or imagined, might well have come to pass in any event, as part of what is commonly referred to as Progress; but that they were hastened along by the persistent agitation of Mrs. Stanton and Miss Anthony there can be no doubt.

At the time they met, Mrs. Stanton was thirty-five years old, Miss Anthony was thirty-one. But each had since her childhood felt the itch to change the world, and each was by 1851 a veteran gadfly.

Elizabeth Cady Stanton was the daughter of a well-to-do lawyer of Johnstown, New York, who after serving a term in Congress had been elected a judge. She

ANGELS OF WOMAN'S RIGHTS

was one of six children, five girls and a boy, but when Elizabeth was eleven her brother died. Her father was inconsolable. She went into the darkened parlor where he mourned, climbed on his knee, and wondered what she might do to comfort him. They sat in silence. At length, as she recalled later in her reminiscences, he sighed and said: "Oh, my daughter, would that you were a boy!"

Little Elizabeth at once determined to do what she could to remedy this defect. To be learned and to be courageous: that was what was needed. She undertook to study Greek, Latin, and mathematics with a class of boys in the town's academy. Most of them were much older than she, yet after three years she took a prize in Greek. Never had she been so proud. She raced home to show her prize to her father. He seemed pleased. There was an awkward pause while she waited for the word that would show he agreed a daughter could be as good as a son. At last he kissed her forehead. "Ah," he said, "you should have been a boy!"

But even had Judge Cady more nearly approached a child psychologist's ideal of parenthood, his daughter would have found plenty of reason to rebel. There was the law, which made a wife her husband's serf. There was custom, which forbade her to enter college. Moreover, when Elizabeth and some others of the Presbyterian Girls' Club raised money to send a student to a theological seminary and, on his graduation, presented him with a new black broadcloth suit, what did he select as text for his maiden sermon? A verse from the First Epistle of Paul to Timothy: "But I suffer not a woman to teach, nor to usurp authority over the man, but to be in silence." Miss Cady walked out on him.

As it happened, there was a channel at hand for her defiance. Her cousin, Gerrit Smith, was a prominent abolitionist; his house in Peterboro was a station on the Underground Railroad. Events, then, followed on each other with uniform predictability. Naturally at Cousin Gerrit's house she met an impecunious but mettlesome young radical, Henry Stanton, already well-known as an antislavery orator; naturally Judge Cady forbade their engagement; naturally she married

the young man anyway. (Naturally she instructed the clergyman to remove the word "obey" from the ceremony.)

Their wedding trip was to London, where Stanton was a delegate to a world antislavery convention. The young bride was dismayed to find that females, though elected as delegates, were barred from participation, were barred even from fighting against slavery. Wendell Phillips, of the American delegation, argued that Lucretia Mott and the others be permitted to share in the convention's business—but to no avail: the Word of God was invoked against them, and they were obliged to sit in the gallery, William Lloyd Garrison joining them in pointed protest against their exclusion. After that it was only a question of time before Mrs. Stanton would agree with Lucretia Mott and some other Quaker women to call the first woman's rights convention, in Seneca Falls.

Since Mrs. Stanton could write fluently, to her fell

Elizabeth Cady Stanton (left) and Susan Brownell Anthony fought the good fight from their meeting in 1851 until Mrs. Stanton died in 1902. Miss Anthony was the better organizer; her colleague was the more persuasive writer.

19

the task of drafting a Declaration of Sentiments and a clutch of appropriate resolutions. Over much opposition, she insisted on including a resolution that women should fight for the vote. And so it all began.

News of the convention seeped out to the nation. Newspaper editors and preachers were stupended. What was all this? A joke? or a monstrous calamity? They decided it was both; ridicule and anathema alike were hurled at the one hundred men and women who had signed the declaration. One by one names were withdrawn. Too late; the damage had been done. That was in July, 1848, and so by the time she met Miss Anthony three years later, Mrs. Stanton was already a notorious woman. So far was she steeped in feminism that she was caparisoned in the celebrated ultrafeminist short dress and trousers, the costume called bloomers after Mrs. Amelia Bloomer, editor of that dauntless journal of temperance, *The Lily*. It was, indeed, Mrs. Bloomer who introduced Mrs. Stanton to Miss Anthony, a function that seems in retrospect as superfluous as introducing Mutt to Jeff.

Susan B. Anthony had come to this street corner in Seneca Falls by a different route. She was also one of several children, but her father admired and petted her quite as much as he did his other daughters and his two sons. In fact it was he who fostered in young Susan a dedication to reform; he was a reformer himself: a Quaker, an advocate of temperance, an opponent of slavery, and an interested friend in the earliest struggles for woman's rights. Susan, in consequence, early raised the banner of purity. By 1849 Miss Anthony was an official of the Daughters of Temperance and fairly launched on her long career as Miss Fix-it for the commonweal.

"Reform," she wrote to her father, "needs to be the watchword! And someone must preach it who does not depend on the popular nod for his dinner." Her father agreed most heartily; he was, after all, one of the hundred who had signed Mrs. Stanton's Declaration of Sentiments some time before. For *her* dinner, Miss Anthony worked as a schoolmarm, but inevitably this vocation gave way to the avocation of reform. To organize conventions, engage the right speakers, supervise committees, draft the right resolutions, raise money, elect the right officers—my, but all this took time! And especially when no one else could be trusted, not even men. Perhaps, as she was coming to suspect, least of all men.

Men: Miss Anthony was increasingly mistrustful of them. She was not, as a young woman, notably attractive, and she had keen misgivings about her physical appearance, which was marred, she fancied, by a slight strabismus of one eye, a condition that was more noticeable when she was tired; but on the other hand she had never lacked for escorts on moonlit evenings, nor even for proposals of marriage. Clearly she could have made some man a capable, if not remarkably romantic, helpmeet; but as she passed into her fourth decade she resolutely thrust from her all sentimental thoughts. It was not easy. For years her diary would receive her wintry confidences: "Mr. Blank walked home with me; marvellously attentive. What a pity such powers of intellect should lack the moral spine." Had poor Mr. Blank interrupted a talk on committee business to essay a good-night kiss? The diary was not told. At all events, when she first met Mrs. Stanton, Miss Anthony was already a determined spinster, and so she would ever remain.

Almost at once the two went to work on each other. First Miss Anthony got Mrs. Stanton elected president of her Women's State Temperance Society, then Mrs. Stanton prevailed on Miss Anthony to clamber into the bloomer costume and join the struggle for woman's rights. For the next ten years the two campaigned together shoulder to shoulder on one convention platform after another.

And what did they achieve? As to woman's rights, the truth is: not much; at least, not much that can be measured. None came to their conventions save those who were already convinced or those who strenuously desired to shut them up. And yet they were strikingly successful in one way: gradually they transformed a national climate of opinion. Prudent conservatives and thoughtful liberals alike were painfully shoved into an awareness that *something* had to be

This 1869 Currier & Ives lithograph was called The Age of Iron, or Man as He Expects to Be—*after his wife's "emancipation." Today's baby-sitting husband, enmeshed in the toils of "togetherness," may wince at the satirist's acumen.*

done. Not much, surely, the conservatives insisted; perhaps more than we realized, the liberals admitted; but *something*.

And so, like all radical reformers, Mrs. Stanton and Miss Anthony subsisted on hope. No matter how often their hope was dashed, it blithely rose again, a phoenix, to spur them to their next call, appeal, convention, petition, or rally. During this decade Mrs. Stanton bore four children, increasing her tribe to seven. Miss Anthony, on the other hand, protested ever more sharply against what she called "the mighty matrimonial maelstrom." But whatever the problems posed in their personal lives, both Mrs. Stanton and Miss Anthony still held high their hopes for the future.

The Civil War dashed them again. While the men were fighting, clearly they would ignore the rights of women. To Miss Anthony, at least, it almost seemed as if the war had been deliberately concocted as an excuse to avoid facing the paramount issue. Mrs. Stanton's husband, Henry, had been one of the founders of the Republican party, and Miss Anthony's brother Daniel was an early adherent; but the two women were more radical. Leery of Lincoln, they stuck with the abolitionists. Only after the Emancipation Proclamation went into effect, partially freeing the slaves, did they decide to support the war fully: they wrote another Appeal, another Call; they formed another organization, the Women's National Loyal League, of which (naturally) Mrs. Stanton was president and Miss Anthony secretary; they held another convention; they printed more petitions and got more signatures, almost four hundred thousand of them, praying for the unconditional abolition of slavery.

After the war, reform was at a low ebb. Miss Anthony retired to Kansas, where brother Daniel was editor of a Leavenworth newspaper that he aimed to transform into "the most radical mouthpiece" in the state. But at that moment an event occurred that was like battle smoke to an old war horse, and Miss Anthony's nostrils flared. The Fourteenth Amendment to the Constitution had just been proposed, and as her eye ran over the suggested formulation it was suddenly arrested by one phrase: ". . . But when the right to vote . . . is denied to any of the male inhabitants of such State, being twenty-one years of . . ."

Male! The word stiffened her. It was the first time that males had ever dared to introduce the word into their precious Constitution. At once Miss Anthony set in motion plans for her journey home. What was the trouble back east? Where were Lucretia Mott, Lucy Stone, Antoinette Blackwell? Now Miss Anthony was sure there should have been woman's rights conventions right through the war: the last had taken place in 1860 but now it was 1865, and the country had patently gone to sleep. Clanging the tocsin, she headed east, giving speeches all along the way. In Boston she cornered two old friends, Henry Ward Beecher and Theodore Tilton. What was wrong, she asked, with merging the Anti-Slavery Society and the Woman's Rights Society into one grand new organization, the National Equal Rights Association, to fight from one platform for one cause—universal suffrage? Beecher nodded. Tilton nodded. Since Beecher, the pastor of Brooklyn's Plymouth Church, was already a national figure, his consent was significant. That of Tilton, an influential journalist, was perhaps even more important.

But Wendell Phillips dragged his feet. It would, he announced, require three months' notice for the Anti-Slavery Society to change its name. Miss Anthony sent out a similar notice to the members of the Woman's Rights Society. As usual, the two groups planned concurrent conventions in New York; there the job would be done.

Miss Anthony had taken into account everything except the perfidy of the male. For when the motion to merge was proposed at the Anti-Slavery convention, Wendell Phillips blandly ruled it out of order. He was, he declared, opposed to coalition. And at the woman's rights meeting, Phillips spoke of woman suffrage as a goal so far in the future as to be barely discernible. Treachery!

Next day Miss Anthony stalked into the office of the abolitionist journal, *The Anti-Slavery Standard*.

CONTINUED ON PAGE 107

A companion Currier & Ives of the same year, entitled The Age of Brass, or the Triumphs of Womans Rights. *A cowed husband stands at the end of the voting line as a hoydenish Bloomer Girl and a female poll-watcher puff their cigars.*

In this primitive painting Peter Francisco, singlehanded, takes on a Tarleton patrol at Ward's Tavern.

FRANCISCO
the INCREDIBLE

The Revolution's legendary private

could carry a half-ton cannon

or saber a British dragoon in two

By FRED J. COOK

At Brandywine the brave Lafayette was wounded. So, in his baptism of fire, was the sixteen-year-old Peter Francisco.

Wars are fought for the most part by anonymous men who emerge from obscurity, briefly bear the conflict's burden, and then return to their unrecorded ways. Yet every now and then one of them achieves fame in his own right. Such a man, in the war of the Revolution, was Peter Francisco, who became a legend around American campfires, was singled out for praise by Washington, Greene, and Lafayette, and was remembered with honor by his fellow Virginians until his death, long years after independence was won.

His story, mysterious and romantic enough for the pen of a Dumas, began on a morning in early June, 1765, when a four-year-old boy was put ashore by a strange ship at City Point, now a part of Hopewell, Virginia. The boy, large for his age, was swarthy and handsome, with black hair and snapping black eyes. His suit was soiled and badly worn, but the fabric and the cut, the presence of lace about collar and cuffs, indicated that it had been of good quality. Quality, too, was to be seen in the handsome silver buckles of his shoes, each fashioned to spell out the initials "P. F."

Sailors and dock hands tried to question the boy, but they soon found that they could not understand him nor he them. The lad spoke a foreign gibberish—a mixture of Portuguese, French, and Spanish, it was later said; of English, he understood only a few words. He was taken to the Prince George poorhouse, where parish authorities cared for him while trying to find him a home.

His story soon spread through the countryside. It intrigued Judge Anthony Winston, an uncle of Patrick Henry, who investigated, found himself attracted by the mysteriously abandoned boy's appearance, and removed him a mile east of New Store on the old stage road between Lynchburg and Richmond in Bucking- ham County. Here a Negro maid cared for him, and here he lived and worked and grew, his status that of a poor family relation.

As the boy learned to speak English, he searched the vague memories of his childhood and tried to explain to Judge Winston what had happened to him. He was sure of just one thing—his name, Peter Francisco. As for the rest, he had a dim memory of living in a great mansion and playing with a little sister in a lovely garden. His mother was a vague and beautiful vision in his mind. He could remember little about her except that she spoke French. His father was an even more shadowy figure. He spoke a different language than the mother, the boy felt sure, but that was about all he could recall.

Only the final scene of his life at home had registered unforgettably upon his mind. One day as guests were assembling in the great house for dinner, Peter and his sister had been sent out of the way into the garden, enticed by candy and cakes and toys. They were playing there when suddenly some roughly clad men burst in upon them, seized them, and started to carry them away. The little girl struggled and cried out; she managed to wriggle free and escaped. Young Peter was manacled, blindfolded, and gagged. When he was finally released, he was on board a ship. The voyage lasted a long time—until the day he was put into a longboat and rowed ashore at City Point.

Such was the mystery. What could it possibly mean? Long years later, researches abroad by a descendant of Peter Francisco seemed to suggest a reasonable hypothesis.

There was in Portugal in the eighteenth century a noble family named Francisco. At one time, the head of the house became entangled in some unsuccessful political machinations. The penalty for political failure in those days was usually the head of the offender, but in this instance a more diabolical punishment was decreed: the father should see his young son beheaded.

The house of Tory Benjamin Chew was an important British strong point at Germantown, Francisco's second battle.

The British reduced Forts Mercer and Mifflin to open the Delaware River. Francisco was among the survivors at Mifflin.

Before the sentence could be carried out, however, the boy suddenly and mysteriously disappeared. Records that would have established his name and the names of his parents had been lost; but the dim outlines of the story suggest that Peter Francisco may well have been the son and that his parents may have arranged for his kidnapping and transportation to America.

This possible solution of the riddle was unknown at the time, however, and the boy grew up on Judge Winston's estate, set apart from the common run of man both by the mystery of his past and the awesome power of his rapidly developing physique. From the first he helped around the forge, and as he grew he developed the skill and muscles of a smith. While still in his teens he attained his full stature: 6 feet 6 inches and 260 pounds of energy and muscle. Judge Winston had come to love the young giant like a son and made plans to adopt him formally; but before this could be done, the colonial world of America was turned upside down by revolution.

Judge Winston represented Buckingham County in the Virginia Convention and was one of the patriot leaders. On March 23, 1775, young Peter Francisco listened entranced as Patrick Henry, his benefactor's nephew, delivered his impassioned "give me liberty, or give me death!" War was just a step away.

Peter Francisco, though he was only fourteen, wanted to enlist immediately. His eagerness was in keeping with his character. In normal times, he had much of the huge man's placidity of temperament; but exigencies aroused in him the strong man's pride of strength. Judge Winston, more cautious and conservative, considered him too young and made him promise to wait a year. When the time expired, nothing could hold Peter Francisco longer at Hunting Towers; he enlisted in the celebrated Tenth Virginia Regiment as a private, and marched off to war.

He first saw action on September 11, 1777, on the desperate field of Brandywine, the little stream south of Philadelphia along which Washington tried to check the advance of Howe's army. With a circular flanking movement reminiscent of his tactics on Long Island, Howe surprised the Americans, who were expecting a frontal assault. The Tenth Virginia and other fresh regiments were rushed on the field late in the day in an effort to protect the rear and halt the fierce British advance.

Peter Francisco and his comrades in the Virginia line were stationed in a place called Sandy Hollow, a narrow defile flanked by woods. British troops were pursuing the fleeing Continentals along the road through the narrow pass, and the Tenth Virginia was one of the regiments given the job of blocking their path. With the Marquis de Lafayette galloping furiously back and forth across the battlefields, with Washington himself spurring up to the front to inspire his troops, the Virginians and detachments of the Pennsylvania line fought for forty-five stubborn, bloody minutes against the overwhelming weight of the victory-flushed British. Their desperate stand in the wooded defile of Sandy Hollow saved an army. Washington was beaten, but he still had a force capable of fighting again.

Two of those who had stood out in the fierce melee met for the first time after the fighting was over. One was Lafayette, who had drawn all eyes by his reckless dashes across the fire-swept field; the other was the sixteen-year-old giant who had towered above his fellows of the Virginia line. Both had been wounded by British musket balls, and both were treated at the home of a Quaker near the battlefield. Lafayette drew Francisco into conversation, the first tentative step in what was to become a lifelong, enduring friendship.

The Brandywine wound, the first of a series Peter Francisco was to suffer, did not keep him long from

In the melee at Monmouth, where Washington relieved blundering Lee to save the day, Francisco was wounded again.

He was also in the van as Anthony Wayne stormed Stony Point, stopping Sir Henry Clinton's drive on West Point.

24

the front. Less than a month later he was in a battle again, at Germantown, and he went straight from this futile attack on Howe's entrenchments to an even more desperate trial in defense of the American forts that guarded the lower Delaware and prevented the British from reinforcing their garrison in Philadelphia.

The main American defense line was composed of channel obstructions and the guns of two forts: Fort Mercer, at Red Bank on the New Jersey shore, and Fort Mifflin, directly opposite on Mud Island in the middle of the river. Peter Francisco was among the 450 men assigned to the defense of Fort Mifflin, a post that should have been garrisoned by at least 1,000.

After being repulsed at Fort Mercer, the British turned their attention to the much more vulnerable Fort Mifflin on its exposed island. Their formidable bombardment reduced the fort to ruins, and even the uninjured among the defenders were almost stupefied from the shelling and on the verge of collapse from exposure and lack of sleep. Among these fortunate few, who escaped to the New Jersey shore under cover of darkness, was Peter Francisco.

The following June found him on the battlefield of Monmouth, where he received his second wound, a serious one, from a British musket ball. The effects were to bother him the rest of his life, but the pain and the narrow escape failed to slake his appetite for war. A year after Monmouth, in the summer of 1779, he was back as a private in the Virginia line, ready to take part in the storming of the strong British outposts at Paulus Hook and Stony Point—where Francisco participated in a fierce, commando-like charge and received his third wound of the war.

Having served out his last enlistment, Peter Francisco returned to Virginia. But he promptly volunteered again, this time in a militia regiment headed by Colonel William Mayo of Powhatan County.

Never had the plight of the embattled patriots in the south been so desperate. Savannah and Charleston had fallen, and the Continental Congress was attempting to assemble a new army under a new commander in the hope of driving the British out. It was a slender hope at best, but the Congress, in its ineffable wisdom, picked the one commander for the Southern Department who could be counted on to insure disaster. He was the incompetent intriguer, Horatio Gates, his reputation bloated by the success earned for him by better men at Saratoga.

The fatuous Gates took command of a disorganized conglomeration of men in rags and tatters, desperate even for food. Disdainful of reality, he assumed the offensive. He kept insisting to his aides that he had command of an army of 7,000 men, and he refused to listen when one of the most capable officers in the south, Otho Williams, his deputy adjutant general, tried to show him that actually only 3,052 were present and fit for duty. Relying sublimely on the 4,000 phantom fighters who existed only in his own deluded mind, Horatio Gates blundered south to strike Cornwallis at Camden, South Carolina.

Never in the entire war did Cornwallis have so easy a task. Instead of waiting to be struck, he struck first. The earliest premonition of disaster came on the sultry, moonless night of August 15, 1780. Banastre Tarleton, Cornwallis' almost psychopathically cruel cavalry leader, surprised Armand's Legion—Gates's advance scouting force—smashed it, and drove it in upon the First Continental Brigade. Soon all was confusion. The Americans, who had been on a night march toward the enemy, halted and huddled together; the British withdrew temporarily and prepared to launch their thunderbolt.

It exploded at dawn. The full force of the attack fell on the American left, where the Virginia militia was stationed. There were few veterans like Peter Francisco among them. By far the great majority had never

CONTINUED ON PAGE 92

At Camden the British cut the fleeing Americans to pieces. Francisco saved his colonel—and an 1,100-pound cannon.

At Guilford, here seen in the winter, Francisco cut down eleven Britishers—and suffered a near-fatal wound himself.

In such periaugers as this, early ferry operators handled New York's harbor traffic.

D uring more than two and a half centuries New York was pre-eminently the City of Ferries. Never was a city more dependent on them. Decade after decade, generation after generation, they lurched and lumbered and tooted raucously along the scores of miles of New York's water front, seemingly permanent parts of the metropolitan scene. Observing them, one fascinated out-of-towner exclaimed: "They're like big houses detaching themselves from one side of the harbor, drifting across it, and attaching themselves to the other side." In the two world wars, Europe-bound American soldiers from inland parts of the United States who had never seen the sea mistook the ferries for the transports that were to carry them across the ocean.

As early as 1846 there were eleven regular ferry lines serving Manhattan, Long Island, Staten Island, and New Jersey. There were fifteen lines in 1850; and, by 1910, the map of lower Manhattan, from Central Park down, showed thirty-five different routes, each employing a small or large flotilla of boats, constantly progressing in size and comfort and up-to-the-minute appointments. They ran at intervals of from five to sixty minutes. Various railroads terminating in Jersey City or Hoboken or on Long Island soon started operating ferries in connection with their trains—and two of them are still reluctantly doing it. Some of the ferry companies maintained a twenty-four-hour schedule. It was, be it remembered, a blissful age when any point on the East Coast could be reached by steamship and when *ten* lines were engaged in serving the upper Hudson River alone.

In addition to all this there were, and still are, ferries, run by municipal and federal agencies, between Manhattan and the various small islands roundabout. At the apex of New York City's ferry age the scores of

Before tunnels and bridges reduced the vast flotilla

BOATS

Steam arrived in 1811, and Fulton's dou-ble-hulled Brooklyn ferry began in 1814.

ferryboats engaged in these multiple services gave a color and originality to its harbor that made it unique among the great ports of the world.

First among New York's ferries was the one established in 1638 or thereabouts between Peck Slip in Manhattan, and Brooklyn, then one of the fast-growing Dutch settlements on Long Island. The impresario of this service, a Dutchman, Cornelis Dircksen, used to work on his little farm nearby until somebody seized with a craving to go to Brooklyn blew a horn hanging from a tree at Peck Slip, whereupon Cornelis exchanged farming for ferrying. (At the Brooklyn end another horn hanging from another tree mobilized another ferryman.) At first Cornelis and his successors employed rowboats and canoes; later, larger craft with sails replaced them.

The steady growth of New Amsterdam and neighboring settlements on Long Island and Staten Island and in New Jersey was bringing proportionate development to the transportation business. In 1661, a ferry was started between the Battery and Bergen on the Jersey shore; and another, in 1667, across the Harlem River. The latter waterway soon had a bridge across it, thus ending Manhattan's complete isolation by water from the rest of the world. But all the other sides of the island remained ideal for profitable ferrying ventures.

TEXT CONTINUED ON PAGE 30

This high-flying bird's-eye view of New York, lithographed just a century ago by John Bachman, underlines the reason why insular Manhattan needed so many ferries. No bridges linked it with Brooklyn (center right) or the other settlements farther north on Long Island (upper right) or with the Jersey shore (left). Most of the narrow Harlem River to the north was unbridged as well. Today, however, only to the southward is the sole direct route by water—to Staten Island (bottom) and the islets in the Upper Bay. Harbor shipping is much reduced, both in numbers and elegance of appearance.

to a fragment, travel was pleasanter, and often faster

The first New York "fferry," as the old records have it, began plying from Manhattan to Brooklyn about 1638. One summoned the operator, Cornelis Dircksen, from his plow with a blast of the horn he hung on a tree (left). The price was three stivers wampum. Choleric Peter Stuyvesant, irritated by the delays, soon nationalized the service. In 1661, another Dutchman named Jansen commenced a similar ferry, with extra oars for hurried travelers, across the Hudson. He had to carry the Governor free. And thus several important ferrying characteristics were early established: loud tooting noises, low prices, government interference, and free-loading officialdom. They remain to this day.

Near the humble setting at left, a ferry service launched one of America's great fortunes. With a hundred dollars extracted from his parents' slender savings, Cornelius Vanderbilt in 1806 commenced a ferry service from Staten Island by sail to Manhattan and prospered very greatly. But the idea that really altered the life of the sprawling seaport was steam; it ended oars and sail and the "team-boats" in which patient horses treadmilled scows and flatboats across the waters. In 1811 Robert Fulton and his partner, Chancellor Robert Livingston, introduced steam ferries between the Battery and the Jersey shore. And by about 1838, when Nicolino Calyo painted the steamer Hoboken, above, the outline of the modern ferry was already beginning to emerge.

28

Elegant Steam Power

Displaced Oars and Sail

The Jersey City *(above), which ran between Cortlandt Street, Manhattan, and Jersey City in the 1850's, already possessed, like the* Fulton *in the Currier & Ives below, most of the handsome characteristics of the ferry at its finest stage of design. She was double-ended, high-stacked for a hot fire and speed, and was 208 feet long, only a few feet shorter than Jersey ferries today. In later years the walking beam disappeared, followed by the paddle wheels and, as the owners' pride subsided, the gay pennants and the bright paint.*

Below is the ladies' cabin, all cream and gold paint and ma-hogany furniture, on the iron steamer Bergen *of the Hobo-ken Ferry Company, the sensation of 1889; she was the first double-end propeller boat as well. This kind of spacious, slightly overblown elegance, grown shabby in recent years, still marks the older vessels now operating on the Lacka-wanna and Jersey Central lines. The "stream-lined" boats purchased lately by a city government unburdened with taste are simply utilitarian and ugly. The doom of the ferry, of course, was spelled by the bridges and tunnels. Yet even after the Brooklyn Bridge came into use (right) in 1883, the Fulton Ferry, below, struggled manfully on for 40 years.*

Harper's Weekly, JANUARY 5, 1889; CULVER SERVICE

Soon the city authorities got busy drafting rules and regulations. Ferrymen were forbidden to operate without a license. They were required to provide proper "servants"—*i.e.*, crews and other employees—to "pass all officials free," and to refrain from navigating in stormy weather. The charge for the ferriage of a two-horse wagon was twenty stivers, or one dollar; for a one-horse wagon, sixty cents. The regular fare for each passenger was fifteen cents; but, for some mysterious reason, Indians were charged thirty cents. Ferry operators were obligated to shelter patrons in houses at each terminus of their lines—a wise regulation, since interruptions of service before the days of steam sometimes lasted twenty-four hours or more.

Ferrying by sail laid the foundations of a fortune for **Cornelius Vanderbilt**, who won his title of Commodore from it, and it promised another to Robert Fulton, who obtained permission in 1811 to run two vessels built by him, equipped with steam-driven ma-

chinery of his own invention, as ferries between the Battery and the Jersey shore. A year later, he and his wealthy partner, Robert Livingston, were authorized to operate another line across the East River to Long Island.

Fulton's steam ferryboats were of the catamaran type, with two hulls, united by a primitive bridge, or deck. They had a steering wheel between the hulls and a rudder at each end. The machinery he devised for them was placed on the deck amidships. Both ends of the boats were alike, making it possible for them to function without turning around. All that was needed to move them in the opposite direction was to reverse the machinery. This has remained a feature of New York's ferryboats to the present day, although side-wheelers gave way after a time to propeller-driven craft.

Weather permitting, Fulton's boats could cross from the Battery to Jersey in fourteen minutes—their average time was twenty minutes—a great improvement

on the forty-five minutes' average required by sailboat ferries.

Seventy-six years ago the fateful handwriting on the wall for New York's ferryboat era became clearly visible to all whose minds could interpret correctly what their eyes saw. In 1883 the Brooklyn (or, more properly, East River) Bridge was opened to traffic. Soon, in the wake of the East River Bridge, came the Manhattan and the Williamsburg and the Queensborough and the Hell Gate bridges, and, on the Hudson,* the George Washington Bridge. Finally, the huge Triborough Bridge linked Bronx, Queens, and Manhattan. Subway tunnels were dug, one close after the other, through

* To the confusion of visitors, New Yorkers sometimes call the Hudson the North River, although it lies to the west. The waterway at the north, the Harlem River, is really a strait, and so is the East River, in reality the western outlet of Long Island Sound. We could go on to point out that the Upper Bay is below Manhattan, that Jackson Heights are quite low, and that Turtle Bay is dry land—but this perhaps will suffice. [Ed.]

which trains roared to Long Island and New Jersey, and vehicular tunnels further robbed local ferries of the lucrative carrying of passengers and vehicles. The Pennsylvania Railroad drove its great tubes under the Hudson River and beyond it under the East River, linking New Jersey, Manhattan, and Long Island on a through route. Trains from the South and West could pass without interruption into New York and thence (via Long Island and its great Hell Gate Bridge to the mainland) into New England. This superseded the huge train-ferry boat *Maryland*, which had long transported passengers from Boston and the rest of New England across New York Harbor to trains for Philadelphia and Baltimore and Washington.

How they used to line her decks as she steamed along the East River in daylight; how they gaped at the wonderful panorama of color and movement and beauty and power spread before them; and, at night, with what awe they contemplated an equally breath-taking

CONTINUED ON PAGE 78

31

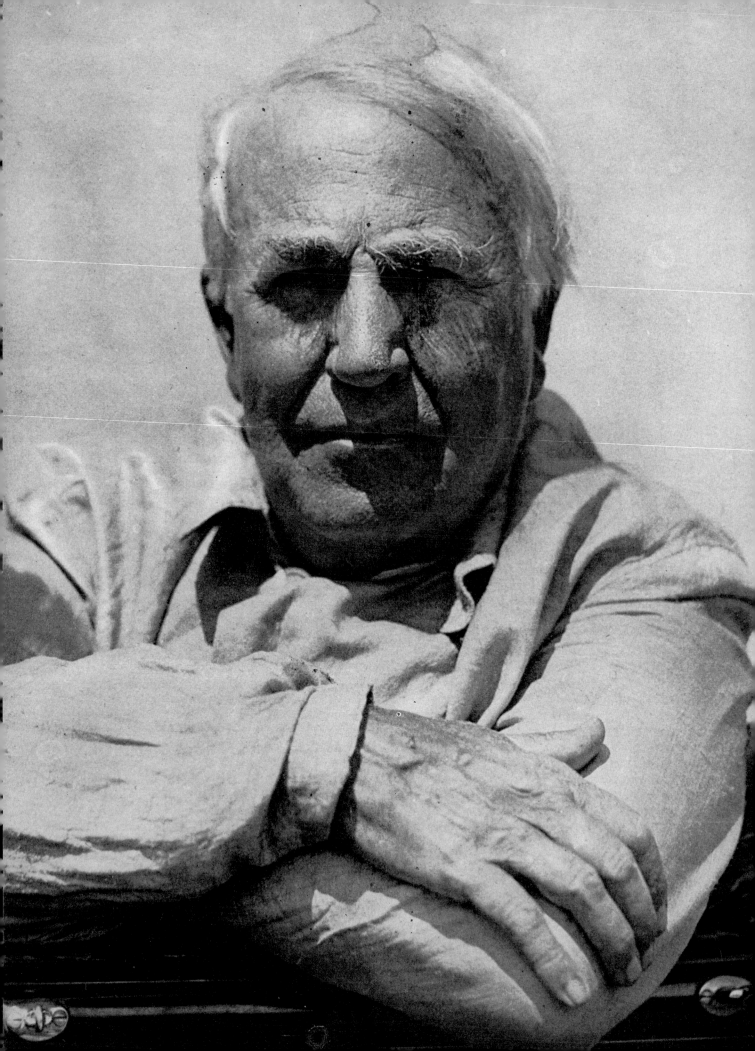

EDISON:
Last Days of the Wizard

By MATTHEW JOSEPHSON

Few Americans have been idolized more in their own lifetime than Thomas Edison, the self-educated "wizard" of practical science, whose countless inventions—among them automatic telegraph systems, electric generators, storage batteries, the phonograph, and the first practical incandescent lamp—have so irrevocably altered our civilization. What follows is an account of Edison's busy old age, when his every movement seemed to the public the fulfillment of a legend. It is taken from Matthew Josephson's major biography, due this month from McGraw-Hill.

It was only after the turn of the century that the electrical age really arrived in America. Just prior to that time, through the nineties, the country as a whole, save for a few luminous city districts, still lived by the smoky glow of oil lamps or by gaslight. Then, thanks to long-distance transmission, power stations mushroomed everywhere.

Electricity gave a new tempo and a new character to all industry. It was easily carried across mountain barriers and rivers from power sites and converted into a multitude of uses. The ponderous steam-powered mills of the nineteenth century had been darkened by their huge belts and shafts. Now the electric motor permitted the greatest flexibility in the design of the factory. The introduction of electric motors into assembly-line operations during the early decades of the century, as at Henry Ford's Highland Park plant, had the effect of raising industrial efficiency by about fifty per cent.

When men looked about them they saw that the

At seventy-one, Thomas Edison was still vigorous and alert. His roughhewn features were known to millions, for in his lifetime he became an acknowledged American folk hero.

buildings of their cities reached toward the clouds, because of the electric elevator; that thousands of electric streetcars and railway cars carried them about with an unheard-of ease and convenience; that incandescent lights blazed everywhere. And when they contemplated these changes they thought with one accord of plain Thomas A. Edison. That other brilliant inventors coming after him had developed high-voltage transmission, and an A.C. motor adaptable to manifold industrial use, mattered little. Leadership in inaugurating the electrical age was almost universally attributed to Mr. Edison.

Edison's legendary success story, like his expressive physiognomy—reproduced millions of times on his cylindrical records—was familiar to all men. In short, he was almost universally regarded as one of the real "makers" of America, well-suited to serve as a folk hero of modern times.

He had gained both weight and girth as he grew older, yet kept them under control. With his big head, white hair, inky-black eyebrows and large pale countenance, clad soberly in dark clothes, with a rolled-collar shirt and string necktie, he could pass easily for an old American worthy out of the early years of the Republic.

The story of the intimate friendship between Henry Ford and Edison forms an important chapter in both men's later careers and strongly illuminates the special qualities of each. They were similar in social origin and background, shared many interests in common, and yet were strikingly different in mind and temperament. Ford was extremely sentimental; he kept the most trivial memorabilia of his boyhood days and loved rustic dances, old tunes, and country folkways, in which he tried to revive interest among the helots of the assembly lines. Though one of the chief architects of the machine age, he amused himself by re-creating at immense cost an old-fashioned country village in Dearborn, such as he had known in his youth. He was endowed with a fine engineering talent as well as a fierce will to power; nevertheless he was an exceedingly simple being at bottom, and dangerously ignorant.

Since their first encounter in 1898, when Ford was still an employee of the Edison Illuminating Company in Detroit, the automobile magnate had regarded Edison with a reverence that was almost superstitious. Their next meeting came about ten years later, in 1909, when Ford was embroiled in his long court fight to break the monopoly of the Detroit manufacturing group that owned the automobile engine patents of G. B. Selden. At a critical point in this affair, Ford is said to have walked in on Edison at his laboratory, unannounced, to seek his advice. The Model T was under way, and the future of his mass production plans depended on his decision. Edison advised him to stay out of the automobile trade association and fight their licensing monopoly. When Ford triumphed over his opponents in court in 1911, he felt again that the old inventor had guided him well.

Edison called him "Henry"; but Ford never addressed the inventor save as "Mr. Edison." Edison was quick of thought and speech, while Ford was a dull talker. At first the older man had felt the other to be something of a simpleton, but after a while he said he

was "afraid of him, for I find him most right where I thought him most wrong."

In friendship, Ford could be most generous. Late in 1912, he decided to equip his austere black T-model, up to then started by a hand-crank, with a storage battery, self-starter, and electric lamps. His first thought was to use Edison batteries, and he soon contracted for a big supply of them. "I will design a starter, new dynamo, motor, new rigging and proper battery," Edison wrote in a letter of agreement in 1914. If tests proved the mechanism satisfactory, the Edison Storage Battery Company was to manufacture one hundred thousand battery-generator sets especially patterned for the Ford car. To finance this undertaking the Ford Motor Company advanced $1,150,000 on account.

The Edison alkaline battery, however, showed a relatively low voltage and did not function well in circuit with an automobile self-starter; Ford was as keenly disappointed as Edison in these results. Then, still eager to help his friend, Ford undertook to build a small electric car powered by the Edison batteries he had already ordered. After visiting Edison in Florida in the winter of 1915, he returned to Detroit to find his engineers experimenting with an electric car designed to be driven by ordinary lead-acid batteries. According to his assistants, "he raised the devil. . . . They weren't to build a car for lead batteries; they were to use Edison batteries, he insisted." But the Edison battery proved to be inadaptable for such use, and by mutual agreement was abandoned.

At the same time their relations continued to be intimate on other than business grounds. In February, 1914, Mr. and Mrs. Ford had first come to Edison's winter retreat in Fort Myers for a long visit. Under the tutelage of the naturalist John Burroughs, Ford had become so enamored of nature studies that on returning from a journey to England he had brought with him a collection of 380 songbirds, with which he hoped to stock America's forests. On this occasion Burroughs was invited to join Edison and Ford in southern Florida. "We'll go down to the Everglades and revert back to Nature," the inventor promised. "We will get away from fictitious civilization."

Between them Edison and Ford had done more perhaps than any other living men to foster, if not a fictitious civilization, then a highly mechanized one, and its mass culture. There was a touching incongruity, therefore, in their tour of the Everglades and the cypress forests, under the guidance of John Burroughs, in their bird-watching and their examination of exotic flowers. In those days the tall, thin, bearded Burroughs, "a philosopher who worshiped God's truth in Nature," by his pen and his example led mankind to

Edison's New Jersey home, Glenmont.

the outdoors. Ford enjoyed himself so heartily that not long afterward he bought a winter home near Edison's.

In 1915, when Edison and Ford were visiting the Panama-Pacific International Exposition at San Francisco, Ford took Edison, together with Harvey Firestone, out to Luther Burbank's plantation at Santa Rosa. The inventor had long admired the work of the California botanist, and now conceived the idea of "botanizing" for himself in the beautiful gardens surrounding his Florida home. As with other wise old men, it was to be the happy recreation of his late years.

His own methods of experimentation, he pointed out, were similar to those followed by Luther Burbank. "He plants an acre and when it is in bloom he inspects it and picks out a single plant, of which he saves the seed. He has a sharp eye and can pick out of thousands a plant that has promise of what he wants." From this Burbank could propagate an improved variety with fair certainty of success. That was the essence of Edison's empirical method in chemical research.

During the California trip, Edison, who found touring the countryside in an open automobile a splendid distraction, made plans with Ford, Burroughs, and Harvey Firestone, Ford's supplier of rubber tires, to go on a long camping trip by automobile through New England and New York State during the following summer. Edison himself made all the logistic arrangements for their trip, providing for a "six" touring car to carry the party and a T-model Ford truck to follow it, bearing tents and camping equipment, camp servants and drivers. At the last moment, owing to the pressure of business affairs, Ford found himself unable to join that first expedition, which was a fairly short and simple affair. Edison, accompanied by Firestone, left West Orange on August 28, 1916, and stopped overnight in the Catskill Mountains, after covering eighty-two miles of unpaved country road; then, joining Burroughs the next day at his homestead in Roxbury, New York, he went on with him along the shore of Lake George, over the Adirondacks, to upper Vermont, and then returned home after ten days on the road. Edison always sat up in front with the driver. No matter how rough the road or how deep the holes, he enjoyed bouncing along at speeds up to forty miles an hour, and never showed fatigue. The "shaking out" was good for him, he believed. Burroughs, who was seventy-nine and very bony, pointed out that Edison could bear the jolts because he was "well-cushioned."

Burroughs had suffered from the bad roads and the vibrations of the automobile, but thanks to Edison's stories, he said, he had enjoyed "vibrations and convulsions . . . in the diaphragm around the campfire at night." He gives a diverting picture of Edison in the Adirondack Mountains playing prospector, put-tering about with a little hammer with which he broke up pieces of granite and feldspar. Ah! there was a possible source of potash, if only it could be extracted economically! Burroughs continues:

It was a great pleasure to see Edison relax and turn vagabond so easily, sleeping in his clothes and dropping off to sleep like a baby, getting up to replenish the fire at daylight or before, making his toilet at the wayside creek or pool. . . . One cold night, you remember, he hit on a new way of folding his blankets; he made them interlock so and so, got into them, "made one revolution" and the thing was done. Do you remember with what boyish delight he would throw up his arms when he came upon some particularly striking view? I laugh when I think of the big car two girls were driving on a slippery street in Saranac . . . and when they put on the brakes suddenly, how the car suddenly changed ends and stopped, leaving the amazed girls looking up the street instead of down. Mr. Edison remarked: "Organized matter sometimes behaves in a strange manner."

Edison's laboratory at West Orange.

The next "gypsy" tour took place two years later, in the summer of 1918, after the war had taken a favorable turn. This time Ford made it his business to join Edison, Burroughs, and Firestone, and was very much present at all their subsequent trips to what they called "Nature's laboratory."

Unfortunately the newspapers, with hue and cry, soon followed the wanderings of "America's Most Useful Citizen" and his friend, the flivver king, from one campsite to another, on that second trip. To Edison's annoyance, reporters persistently intruded themselves between him and the panorama of mountains and valleys to press their queries about his war machines, or to describe or photograph him as he cooked potatoes over the fire or took a siesta.

That second camping tour had been organized by Ford and Firestone on a much more elaborate scale than the first, and its itinerary had been publicly announced in advance. The "irrepressible boy of seventy-one," eager for his annual "shaking out," hurried off to pick up John Burroughs in the Catskills, then sped on to Pittsburgh to meet Ford and Firestone. The itinerary for this journey was longer and took them through the Great Smoky Mountains.

Clad in linen dusters and soft caps, they roared along in their motor caravan, startling the sleepy mountain hamlets of West Virginia and North Carolina. Soon they were in deep forgotten valleys where the country people sometimes gathered in little knots to stare at them as they stopped. Some of these people had never seen an electric light, but they knew and recognized Edison as "Mr. Phonograph." On one occasion Henry Ford was evidently discomfited when no one seemed to have heard of him or even to have seen any motorcars before. "Good," said Edison, "we shall have a good time here."

When they pitched their camp in an open meadow, Firestone and the bustling Ford would sometimes engage in a scything match or a "cradling" contest. Edison, however, as Burroughs recalled, was content to settle down in his car and read or meditate, while Ford swung an axe to cut wood for their campfire. To be sure, there were numerous attendants about them now, a luxurious kitchen truck and several supply trucks, providing a sybaritic fare which poor John Burroughs had never known on his own camping trips.

Like many another philosopher Edison could be found acting in complete contradiction to his own professed doctrines. In his journal for the 1919 camping trip, Burroughs wrote:

O Consistency, thy name is not Edison! Ten A.M. Edison not up yet—the man of little sleep! He inveighs against cane-sugar, yet puts two heaping teaspoonfuls into each cup of coffee, and he takes three or four cups a day. He eats more than I do, yet calls me a gourmand. He eats pie by the yard and bolts his food.

While Henry Ford pretended to flee "the artificial life of commercialism" in a motor caravan out in the open country, a spirit of crass commercialism day by day pervaded his well-advertised camping tours. Movie news cameras and publicity agents, who carried on promotion stunts of all sorts, gathered in the train of the Edison-Ford-Firestone motor caravan, which by 1919 boasted fifty cars. Politicians arrived—on one occasion even a President of the United States, Warren Harding—to bask in the limelight of its campfire. Trucks followed behind, bearing large placards reading: *"Buy Firestone Tires."* When the caravan arrived in a community, the festive occasion was exploited by dealers as an opportunity to sell more Ford cars. Henry Ford and Firestone seemed to enjoy it all. But in 1921 John Burroughs died; after that Edison, who was greatly bothered by the crowds, the dust, and all the ballyhoo, decided to come no more.

In those last years the white-haired Edison might have been found more often than not in the gardens of his Florida home, Seminole Lodge, where he remained for a much longer season than formerly. In addition to the thousands of tropical plants set out in the grounds around, there was a special botanical laboratory filled with potted plants that he and a staff of botanists were developing from crossbred strains. He too was botanizing; but as always there was a practical object in view.

Rubber had recently become one of the most important commodities for the modern industrial world, thanks to the automobile. It was produced in distant tropical regions, and in wartime became scarce and extremely dear; during the First World War its price had risen from about twenty cents to more than two dollars a pound. While visiting Burbank's plantation in California together with Ford and Firestone in 1915, Edison had remarked that if the United States entered the war rubber would be the first product to be cut off. Ford had asked him to do something about creating a domestic supply or a substitute, to which Edison replied: "I will—some day."

When rubber became costly again toward 1924–25, owing to the British Far Eastern rubber restriction scheme, Ford and Firestone renewed their pleas that Edison undertake a serious investigation of domestic sources of rubber, which they offered to finance. The Edison Botanic Research Company was thereupon organized in 1927, with the Ford Motor Company and the Firestone Tire & Rubber Company each advancing $93,500 to cover the costs of research, while Edison agreed to contribute his labor. Thus he was engaged in one of his famous "drag-hunts" for some plant, either existing or to be developed by crossbreeding, which contained sufficient rubber latex to be processed for rubber on a large scale.

Of the period that followed, Mrs. Edison said afterward: "Everything turned to rubber in the family. We talked rubber, thought rubber, dreamed rubber. Mr. Edison refused to let us do anything else." Now he was busily "ransacking the world," as his associates reported, gathering and dissecting every class of weed, vine, shrub, and bush that grew.

Prior to a severe illness in 1929 his mental powers showed no perceptible decline. He "got the whole subject of rubber into his head" so he could see every phase of his problem. The main source of supply was the *Hevea brasiliensis,* a tree native to Brazil but successfully transplanted on a large scale to Malaya, Ceylon, and Africa. Coolie labor in the moist equatorial lands had made rubber cheap and abundant, though the rubber tree required five years to mature.

It was well known to scientists that numerous other plants, even those common to the North Temperate Zone, contained caoutchouc latex in varying quantities; the giant milkweed, the southern honeysuckle vine, and shrubs such as the Mexican guayule, already being cultivated in southern California. But the rubber extracted from the guayule was unsatisfactory, being of a highly resinous quality. What Edison hoped to find was a "sowable and mowable" crop native to the United States and capable of being cultivated, harvested, and processed within twelve to eighteen months, so as to provide a source of supply in the event of war or other emergency.

In less than a year Edison reported to Henry Ford that he had collected 3,227 wild plants and shrubs from points ranging from New Jersey to Key West. After flirting with honeysuckle and milkweed, he fixed on the domestic goldenrod as the most promising plant of all.

Goldenrod yielded about five per cent latex. Edison selected the varieties that seemed most promising, divided the roots, planted them separately, divided them again, and crossbred. It was time-consuming; but a giant goldenrod about fourteen feet tall yielding about twelve per cent latex was ultimately developed. Ford was so greatly encouraged by Edison's reports that he purchased an extensive acreage in southern Georgia for the raising of goldenrod.

In the late summer of 1929, while at Glenmont, his home in West Orange, New Jersey, Edison fell ill; his whole digestive apparatus seemed affected and there was some indication of kidney malfunction and of diabetes. But he rose from his bed saying: "Give me five years and the United States will have a rubber crop." But who, now, could give Edison five years?

Oddly enough, not only Edison, but Henry Ford, the Du Pont company, and Standard Oil of New Jersey, after 1925 had received information about the new German chemical process for converting coal or petroleum derivatives into synthetic rubber of the butadiene and sodium type, which was already perfected by the I. G. Farben Gesellschaft around that time. But large-scale operations were not to be carried out until a decade later, prior to World War II. Edison also might have turned his eyes in this direction—which was to be the most profitable for systematic research—but for the fact that the synthetic process was known to require an enormous investment in special chemical plants, which even our biggest rubber tire and chemical corporations refused to risk at that period.

In 1940 federal government subsidies alone would make synthetic rubber production feasible. In that year government scientists thoroughly explored the alternate possibilities of using organic materials available to us, such as Edison's variety of goldenrod and guayule, but reached the conclusion that processing such plants would be more difficult and costly than making a synthetic, and would yield a product inferior to natural India rubber or the new synthetics.

Edison's goldenrod rubber project, therefore, was foredoomed. If Henry Ford suspected this, however, the motor king did not move a hand to stop Edison's dying effort. Where Edison was concerned, the ruthless Ford was all sentiment.

The ninth decade of the inventor's life was a time for the erection of monuments in his honor, a time for the bestowal of medals, ribbons, decorations, and other honorific ornaments that came to him from all quarters of the world. He was touched with bronze; he was as a walking monument himself—in fact, an immortal. People used to come and address him with formal eulogies, generally dilating upon his benefactions to the human race. Solemn little delegations arrived frequently in West Orange, bearing their offerings of plaques or medals, and waited patiently in the library until, as often as not, word came to them that Edison was too busy to accept their gifts in person.

A signal event in Edison's old age was Henry Ford's decision to build an immense museum of the history of industry and invention, as a monument not only to himself but also to his friend Edison, in his native town of Dearborn, Michigan. The untutored man who had once declared in a public courtroom that "History is the bunk," and that he could hire all the historians he wanted, now seemed wholly dominated by his sense of past times, and especially of his own past. He laid out Greenfield Village in Dearborn as a reconstruction of the rural setting of his early life, stuffing it with nineteenth-century farm cottages, churches, and taverns. Here was the jigsaw-styled frame house of a dentist who had been good to him, the original chapel his wife had attended in girlhood, and the little red schoolhouse (probably not authentic) of the lady who had first sung "Mary Had a Little Lamb." Next to the

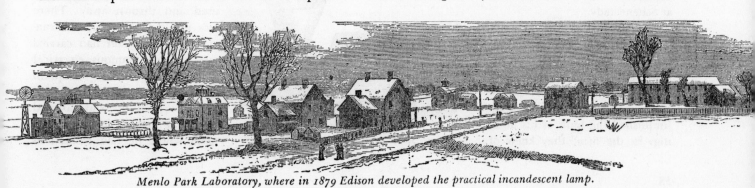

Menlo Park Laboratory, where in 1879 Edison developed the practical incandescent lamp.

nineteenth-century Americana was the vast museum of industry and invention holding everything in the line of machinery, from ancient looms to the giant locomotives of 1925. But over all this reconstruction of the past there loomed the superhuman figure of Edison, whose glory Ford was bent on preserving *in toto*.

Hence Ford began to gather up such relics as he could find of the legendary Menlo Park Laboratory, then in ruins, where Edison had developed his incandescent electric lamp. He not only scoured the New Jersey countryside for the very planks that had fallen off Edison's old sheds, but also gathered together a notable collection of original models of Edison's inventions, installing them in a section of Greenfield Village that was at first known as the Edison Institute. These models were so well restored—or, in some cases, reproduced—that everything worked as before. Wherever he found the debris of Edison's life and labor Ford went digging—even in Fort Myers, where he removed the small electrical laboratory of 1887, by then fallen into disuse.

"Dear me," Mrs. Edison said plaintively one day, when she spied him from her window, scouring about her grounds at Seminole Lodge, "I do wish Mr. Ford would keep out of our backyard!"

Millions were thus lavished by Ford upon his collection of Edisonia alone, the total cost of Greenfield Village being more than $10,200,000. When it was all done, the restored Menlo Park Laboratory stood in its native red New Jersey clay (transported thither by train) and even had a heap of old metal junk lying outside. For had not Edison once said that what the good inventor needed was "imagination and a scrap heap"?

The General Electric Company, at the time, still invoked the name of Thomas A. Edison in its advertising as its founding father, even though he was no longer connected with it. In conjunction with the proposed festival celebrating the fiftieth anniversary of the electric light, planned for October 21, 1929, the great company's executives therefore undertook to sponsor a "colossal" affair to be known and remembered as the "Golden Jubilee of Light." The site selected for the staging of this pageant was the headquarters of General Electric at Schenectady.

Owen D. Young, chairman, and Gerard Swope, president of General Electric, were of the generation after Edison's and had no part in the old controversies of 1892 when the inventor had relinquished the bulk of his holdings in the firm; they knew of

An Edison phonograph.

no animus he might feel against their corporation. There had been, in fact, almost no business relations with Edison's company; but such as they were, as in more recent legal disputes over radio patents, General Electric was, in the opinion of Edison's son Charles, scarcely friendly or helpful. Determined to block General Electric's plan to take over the Jubilee, Charles communicated with Ford and told him of the scheme to "commercialize" Edison's fame. Henry Ford said it was a "shameful action" and promised he would do something about it.

The Ford Museum and Greenfield Village were by then nearing completion. Ford therefore decided to combine the formal dedication of his own institution with the celebration in honor of the electric light. He ordered his builders to rush the job on the great museum building, a vast replica of Independence Hall in Philadelphia, for it was to be the stage setting of the opening-day banquet. Not long after Charles Edison had telephoned him in the early winter of 1929, Ford suddenly appeared in the library of his venerable friend at West Orange and waited for him, walking up and down restlessly, and muttering to himself: "I'll show 'em. I'll kidnap the whole party." Edison agreed to be "kidnapped."

It was a spectacle indeed to see one giant of industry snatching the Golden Jubilee of Light and its hero from the other. Messrs. Young and Swope, greatly taken aback, appealed to Edison and to Ford to accept their original plan, or at least to make it a combined publicity operation. But Edison was unmoved, and Ford was adamant in his desire to have all the trouble and as much of the publicity as possible for himself.

When Edison stepped from the train at Dearborn, two days before the Jubilee was to open, he looked, it was noted, "like a benevolent old wreck," for he had been so gravely ill in August, 1929, with pneumonia, that his life was feared for. Now as he beheld Greenfield Village and the transplanted "Menlo Park," he smiled his broadest smile. Here were all the old bulbs, telegraph instruments and stock tickers, the "Long-Waisted Annie" dynamos, the old generating plant of Pearl Street, New York, and even an old mortar and pestle he had used and thrown away. There was not only the old "tabernacle," where Edison had carried out his most famous electrical experiments, but also the plain boardinghouse across the road from it; even the old railroad station at Mount Clemens, Michigan, where he had worked as a youth, and beside it a reproduction of a little Grand Trunk Railway train, including the baggage car with Tom Edison's little laboratory-on wheels!

An early advertisement for the Edison phonograph.

After Ford had shown him this truly monumental restoration, and asked for his opinion, Edison said: "Well, you've got this just about ninety-nine and one half per cent perfect."

"What is the matter with the other one half per cent?" Ford asked.

"Well, we never kept it as clean as this!" Edison drawled.

President and Mrs. Hoover, and Secretary of the Treasury Andrew Mellon, with attendant secret-service men, arrived on the morning of October 21 at the head of a delegation including the nation's most eminent political and financial personages, among them Owen D. Young, Thomas W. Lamont, J. P. Morgan (the younger), Charles M. Schwab, and Otto H. Kahn; there were also scientists and inventors such as Orville Wright and Madame Curie. As President Hoover approached Detroit in his train, the party was met by Mr. and Mrs. Ford and Mr. and Mrs. Edison at a transfer point, where all changed to a little train out of the Abraham Lincoln era, drawn by a wood-burning locomotive. In this they traveled over a spur line for half a mile to a restored Smith's Creek Junction, where seventy years before Edison was supposed to have been given the bounce out of his baggage-car laboratory. Here a train boy came on with a basket of merchandise; Edison, the onetime newsboy, took it from him and made an effort to walk about for a few moments, crying: "Candy, apples, sandwiches, newspapers!"—offering them to President Hoover. It was absurd, and yet also sheer symbolic drama: the American Dream re-enacted before the world's news cameras. But the principal actor was now feeble and his voice weak.

At nightfall, after all the sights had been displayed to the distinguished guests, Edison appeared on the second floor of the restored Menlo Park Laboratory to demonstrate how he had made a carbonized thread and vacuum globe in 1879 and, at a given moment, turned it on. As many of the guests as could be crowded into the laboratory were on hand to watch Edison re-create an event that seemed by now a scientific fable. Millions more throughout the world were sitting at their radios, listening to the announcer reporting the event:

"The lamp is now ready, as it was a half century ago! Will it light? Will it burn? Edison touches the wire. Ladies and gentlemen—it lights! Light's Golden Jubilee has come to a triumphant climax!"

As the model of the old carbon filament lamp was turned up, all over "Menlo Park," all over Dearborn and Detroit, and in other great cities across the country special lamps blazed up suddenly with an immense yellow refulgence, as the voice on the radio continued:

"And Edison said: *Let there be light!*"

The excitement had been wearing for the old man. But he had more to come. The festival was to be topped off with a banquet for five hundred guests in that inflated model of Independence Hall, a part of the future Henry Ford Museum; Owen D. Young was to be toastmaster, and President Hoover was to give the principal address in dedication of what was afterward called Ford's Old Curiosity Shop. But at the door of the banquet hall Edison faltered and all but collapsed. Led to a settee in the corridor, he sat down and wept, overcome with emotion and fatigue.

"I won't go in," he said to Mrs. Edison. Only she could have overcome his resistance; they brought him some warm milk; he revived a little, entered the hall, and took his place at the seat of honor. Messages from many nations were read, tributes were offered, while he heard nothing and ate nothing.

At the end of the evening Edison spoke briefly but with feeling. He was happy, he said, that tribute was being paid to scientific work:

. . . This experience makes me realize as never before that Americans are sentimental and this crowning event of Light's Golden Jubilee fills me with gratitude. As to Henry Ford, words are inadequate to express my feelings. I can only say to you, that in the fullest and richest meaning of the term—he is my friend. Good night.

Then he slumped into his chair and turned as white as death. Mrs. Edison and President Hoover's physician at once helped him to a room to the rear of the speaker's table, and laid him on a sofa. Drugs were administered and he came to; then he was taken to the Ford home and put to bed for several days. "I am tired of all the glory, I want to get back to work," he said.

He absented himself for longer and longer intervals from his laboratory in the two last years that remained. Only his will seemed to keep him alive, for he ate next to nothing. Often he stayed abed or sat in an easy chair at home, but he still kept in close touch with his technical assistants, who daily brought him news of how the goldenrod-rubber experiments were progressing.

His interest in new "campaigns" never flagged. After meeting Colonel Charles Lindbergh, he insisted on being taken to Newark Airport to learn something about the problems of airplane landing and take-off. "The aviators tell me that they must find a means to see through a fog," he said. "I have an idea about it. I am waiting for a real fog—a water fog—and I will see if I can't penetrate it." Perhaps a rocket would do the trick? In almost his last days on earth Tom Edison was thinking earnestly about rockets, a subject that was to become of great moment to the world a quarter of a century later.

At about this period he ventured the prophecy that "There will one day spring from the brain of Science a machine or force so fearful in its potentialities, so absolutely terrifying, that even man, the fighter who will dare torture and death in order to inflict torture and death, will be appalled, and so will abandon war forever. . . ." He was greatly interested in the impact of Albert Einstein's formulations, but admitted he couldn't understand it. "I am the zero of mathematics," he conceded. In one of his last interviews, he went on to say: "I am much interested in atomic energy, but so far as I can see we have not yet reached a point where this exhaustless force can be harnessed and utilized."

On August 1, 1931, he had a sudden sinking spell and lay near death. He could absorb virtually no food at all—but to the astonishment of his physicians, he rallied and tried to rise from bed again. Since the intense summer heat oppressed him, one of the new air-conditioning machines was installed in his bedroom, and he remained indoors, resting and reading. But as soon as he realized the real state of affairs—that he would never be well enough to go back to work—he seemed to lose the desire to live.

In October, when the sharp-thrusting hills of New Jersey's Orange Valley were daubed in orange, he sank again. In the great library below the hill everyone spoke in hushed tones; the big chair at the huge old roll-top desk was empty; the great carved clock ticked on.

Gloom hung over the mansion in Lewellyn Park. Edison slept, waked a little, and drowsed again, he who had resented every moment lost. As a patient he was both difficult and courageous. There were several eminent medical men attending him, and he persisted in discussing their method of treatment, demanding to know what medicines they were trying and how his body was reacting—and why. His interest in applied science, one might say, never flagged, and ended only with the termination of this "last experiment."

One who ministered to him asked if "he had thought of a life hereafter."

"It does not matter," he replied; "no one knows."

Newspaper reporters maintained a deathwatch in the vicinity of Glenmont day and night. The room upstairs was kept dark at night, with a nurse sitting beside the patient; if the lights went on—then all the world must be told. In the last hours, many of Edison's laboratory associates waited in the hall downstairs, while Charles Edison would go up the great stairway, then down to make his report.

Fifty-two years earlier almost to a day, the men associated with Edison were sitting up with him at night to see how many hours his carbon filament lamp would live. Now his son Charles, after his periodic visits to the sickroom, used the same phrase spoken long ago by the watchers at the Menlo Park Laboratory in October, 1879: "The light still burns."

On October 17 his pulse dropped steeply; in the early morning hours of Sunday the eighteenth, at 3:24 A.M., the lights of his room went on, and the doctors and the nurse came out to announce the end. The electromagnetic telegraph, the telephone, the radio, with all of which his life had been in some way linked, flashed the news to all the corners of the world.

Some thought was given in high places to the idea of honoring his passing in a manner worthy of such a hero's death; the President of the United States, it was proposed, should order all electric current to be turned off for a minute or two in streets, factories, public places, and homes throughout the nation. But no sooner was the thought uttered than it was realized that such action was unthinkable. Because of the very nature of Edison's contribution to the technical organization of modern society, his now-so-vital system of electric power distribution—the blood circulation of the community as it were—would have been arrested; there was risk of incalculable disaster in halting, even for an instant, the great webs of transmission lines and the whole monster mechanism of power that had grown in a half century out of his discoveries. The idea of a momentary "blackout" was therefore abandoned as entirely impracticable. Instead, the President suggested that lights be dimmed voluntarily in private residences, where possible, for a few minutes at 10 P.M. of the day of Thomas A. Edison's funeral. Many paid this last tribute silently, and then the lights were turned on again.

Drawings from Culver Service and Bettmann Archive. Photographs on the following pages from Ford Motor Company, Edison Laboratory National Monument, Firestone Tire & Rubber Company, and Brown Brothers.

On a 1918 camping trip, Edison, Burroughs, Ford, and Firestone (left to right) posed at a ruined gristmill.

EDISON
and his
FELLOW TRAVELERS

It was not surprising that Edison, as the acknowledged patron saint of American industry, numbered among his intimates two leading apostles of the machine age, Henry Ford and Harvey Firestone. On summer jaunts, the three often sought the company of John Burroughs, the naturalist and friend of Walt Whitman. Somehow they never found it incongruous to seek the pleasures of the simple, rustic life that mass production had so much undermined.

HOW'S THAT AGAIN, HENRY? Ford, who once hired Edison

In 1919, the campers posed with their caravan at Green Island, New York.

The nation eagerly followed the camping trips Edison took with Ford, Firestone, and Burroughs from 1914 to 1921. To Edison, these idyls in remote rural areas were a chance to experiment in "Nature's laboratory," away from "fictitious civilization." Unfortunately Ford and Firestone also recognized their publicity value. The once-small caravans grew to mammoth size —the 1919 expedition had 50 cars—and the great men found themselves besieged by an overzealous press. As the ballyhoo got out of hand, and the trips became more circuslike, Edison decided he would come no longer.

ord dressed up for the camera as a western bad man.

In 1921 Ford, Firestone, Edison, and Warren G. Harding (left to right) washed up; Methodist Bishop W. F. Anderson looked on

Ford, Firestone, and Anderson listened as a rumpled Edison discoursed with their fellow camper, President Harding

Seated in early-model sling chairs, Harding and Firestone discussed current events while Edison slept on his good ear

THE CANONIZATION OF EDISON

Unshaven, Edison sat at his desk for this formal portrait.

In his declining years, Edison seemed an almost legendary figure. Newspaper polls voted him "America's most useful citizen"; monuments were erected in his honor, and he was awarded medals by the dozen. Such Edisonian remarks as "Genius is two per cent inspiration and ninety-eight perspiration" became popular maxims. But no man revered Edison more than Henry Ford. The motor king, who busily collected the past for his vast museum at Dearborn, Michigan, spent millions on a reconstruction of the Menlo Park laboratories where Edison had developed the incandescent electric lamp. Ford organized the "Golden Jubilee of Light" celebration at Dearborn, which marked the fiftieth anniversary of Edison's great achievement. On October 21, 1929, dignitaries from all over the world gathered to honor the octogenarian inventor who was, more than any other man, responsible for the age of electricity.

Edison (with cane) looked haggard when he met President Hoover (to his left) at the 1929 "Golden Jubilee of Light."

The aged inventor directs an assistant in his New Jersey laboratory shortly before his death in 1931

"Everybody knew" James Madison was a mediocre leader pushed into the

War of 1812. The facts, his biographer says, suggest a different view

TIMID PRESIDENT?

FUTILE WAR?

By IRVING BRANT

Of all the major events in American history, the War of 1812 is least known to the most people. Its naval glories are exploited in popular narrative. Its military failures, formerly glossed over, are emphasized by more objective historians with something akin to pleasure. Least known of all is the part taken by President Madison, who by virtue of the Constitution was commander in chief of the Armed Forces, charged with the duty of "making" the war that Congress "declared."

Through the years, however, a picture of James Madison has been built up by the brushes or palette knives of historians and popular word-artists. He appears as a pacifistic little man overshadowed by the ample figure of his wife, Dolley; a great political philosopher overwhelmed by the responsibilities of a war into which he was projected, at the age of sixty-one, against his will and with no capacity for executive leadership.

The purpose of this article is to appraise, not to acquit or indict. But in the case of Madison, the adverse preconceptions are embedded so deeply that they stand in the way of a fair appraisal. Historians have rejected the Federalist charge that he carried the United States into war to help Napoleon master the Old World. But with few exceptions they have treated him as the dupe of the French Emperor, tricked into war with England by the apparent repeal by the French of the Berlin and Milan Decrees at a time when both countries were despoiling American commerce. (*See* "If Only Mr. Madison Had Waited," AMERICAN HERITAGE, April, 1956.) As for his conduct of the war, Madison has received little credit for victories and plenty of

blame for misfortunes. Finally, the Treaty of Ghent satisfied none of the grievances cited in the declaration of war, and the one decisive military victory—that of General Andrew Jackson at New Orleans—was won two weeks after the signing of the peace treaty. It all adds up to the picture of a useless and costly conflict, saved by mere luck from being a disaster, and coming to an inconclusive end.

"Everybody knew" in 1812, just as everybody "knows" today, that Madison was timid, hesitant, ruled by stronger men. Everybody knew it, that is, except the foreign diplomats who were sent to overawe him. "Curt, spiteful, passionate," France's Louis Turreau called him. "Madison is now as obstinate as a mule," wrote England's "Copenhagen" Jackson (the Francis James Jackson who in 1807 had burned Denmark's capital) just before the President kicked him out of the country. Turreau's friendlier successor, Louis Sérurier, heard that the Chief of State was ruled by his Cabinet. He waited several months before he wrote to Paris: "Mr. Madison governs by himself."

Expelling an obnoxious minister was a civilian job. But how could Madison be anything of a war leader when "everybody knew" that he had been kicked into the war by Clay, Calhoun, Grundy, and other congressional War Hawks? There were certain things that "everybody" did not know. They did not know that in March, 1809, two weeks after he became President, Madison authorized British Minister David M. Erskine to inform his government that if she would relax her Orders in Council, he would ask Congress "to enter upon immediate measures of hostility against France."

They did not know of a simultaneous notice to France that if she ceased her commercial aggressions and Great Britain did not, "the President of the United States will advise to an immediate war with the latter." Neither Congress nor the public ever learned that when President Madison proclaimed nonintercourse with England on November 2, 1810, he informed General Turreau that continued interference with American trade by England "will necessarily lead to war"—as it did. The 1809 offer to join England against France brought gasps of astonishment in Congress when Madison revealed it in asking for the declaration of war against England. It brought no gasps of any sort from writers of history. It didn't fit their conception of Madison, so they disposed of it by silence.

England first, then France, was Madison's schedule of redress. In August, 1812, the moment he was notified that England had repealed her Orders in Council, he offered to settle the one remaining issue—impressment of seamen—by informal agreement. At the same time he wrote to his minister in Paris that if England made peace and France failed to repair American wrongs, war would be declared against France as soon as Congress convened, and that if England did not make peace he might even recommend a double war. Joel Barlow was directed to show that letter to the French government. As a result, Barlow was called to Poland to confer with Napoleon in the field and complete a treaty, but Napoleon's defeat at Berezina intervened, and Barlow died of pneumonia near Cracow on his way back to Paris. Madison's letter has been in print for nearly a hundred years, ignored even by historians who knew that it was described in the French foreign office as an ultimatum of war.

The same Federalist editors who jeered at "poor Madison" in 1812 denounced him as a dictator in 1814. They were free to do so. Open sedition and silent resistance forced the United States to fight the war with one arm—New England—tied behind her back. That was more crippling than incompetent generals, raw militia, and an empty treasury. Yet the President rejected every counsel that would have narrowed the constitutional liberties of those who gave vocal aid to the enemy. They would hang themselves, he said, and they did. Among all the words of praise addressed to him when he left office, he may have felt keenest pride in those of the Citizens' Committee of Washington:

Power and national glory, sir, have often before been acquired by the sword; but rarely without the sacrifice of civil or political liberty. When we reflect that this sword was drawn under your guidance, we cannot resist offering you our own as well as a nation's thanks for the vigilance . . .

the energy . . . and the safety with which you have wielded an armed force of 50,000 men . . . without infringing a political, civil or religious right.

It takes time, of course, for people to accept a portrait after a hundred years of caricature. At the risk of being abrupt, let us turn to Madison's actions as war leader. Expecting hostilities with England, why did he not call for adequate preparations? He did, but in Congress a vote for taxes was looked on as political suicide. Madison's first action in national defense was to lay up most of President Jefferson's little gunboats as wasteful of men and money in proportion to gunpower and to order laid-up frigates refitted. Congress cut the requested appropriation and stopped the work. In September, 1811, Sérurier told his government that the President was stimulating a nationwide debate on the question of whether it suited the Republic to have a navy, and if so, should it not be "such as can make the American flag respected"? The proposition had to be presented "in this questioning and deferential form," said the Minister, to avoid exciting state jealousy of federal power.

At the ensuing session of Congress the administration asked for twelve seventy-four-gun ships and ten new frigates, and the repair or reconstruction of six of the ten existing frigates. The new construction was voted down and the reconditioning limited to three ships.

To prepare for the land war, which would have to be fought either on American or Canadian soil, the President wanted a quick build-up of military forces. Then, if the expected bad news came from England, the troops would be ready to march on weakly defended Montreal and Quebec before reinforcements could cross the ocean.

With an authorized personnel of ten thousand, the Army had only about four thousand. The President asked that the old regiments be filled up, that ten thousand additional regulars be recruited, and that provision be made for fifty thousand volunteers. Senator William Branch Giles of Virginia, leader of the anti-Madison Democrats, shook the roof as he decried these puny measures. He demanded thirty-five thousand regulars and five-year enlistments, making it necessary to build a large and costly officer corps before men could be recruited. "The efforts of General [Senator Samuel] Smith and of Mr. Giles of Virginia," British Minister Augustus J. Foster reported, "have been added to those of the Federalists as a means to overthrow Mr. Madison and his administration." Congress talked most of the winter and Giles won. The bill for fifty thousand volunteers occasioned a lengthy constitutional harangue and a decision for state-appointed officers. The

CONTINUED ON PAGE 85

John Winthrop, first governor of Massachusetts Bay, founded a "Bible commonwealth" presided over by an elect minority.

Pilgrims and Puritans

Men of a nonconformist faith, they builded firm where others

faltered, and gave New England the character it has never lost

By A. L. ROWSE

The New England Puritans had already behind them almost a century's experience of Protestant effort and thought. What was new, and of extreme importance, was the opportunity to carry these ideas into practice, erect upon the unencumbered soil of the New World a Bible commonwealth free of the corruptions and adhesions of the Old. In this we see a fundamental and continuing element in the American experience, and in America's conception of her role in history.

There can be no doubt at all, after a generation of historical controversy, that the realization of this ideal was the dynamic motive that drove the Puritans across the Atlantic. We might go so far as to say that Charles I and Archbishop Laud made New England; for it was during the decade of personal rule, 1630–40,

and as a consequence of it, that the great migration of many thousands took place.

The Puritans, even in New England, were a minority; a small minority, when one considers effective church membership, which was apt to coincide with full citizenship. All the decisive movements in history are made by minorities. And the Puritans carried with them these irresistible elements of strength, that they knew quite clearly what they wanted, that the character their polity should take was already formulated in their minds and in their writings, the structure of belief and discipline worked out. There were only minor adjustments to be made in accordance with conditions on the other side of the Atlantic, for in the New World, in the wilderness, they were essentially free to have their own way—that was what they

The colony's great preacher, John Cotton, was thought unable to err.

Richard Saltonstall was fined for backsliding, returned to England.

Winthrop's successor, John Endecott, had little use for tolerance.

49

had gone there for. (If they could have had their way at home they would not have gone.) A perfectly clear-minded and determined minority, provided it is agreed and united, can usually impose its will on the rest. Hence, by the way, the emphasis on unity, the determination of Massachusetts to inflict uniformity on all within its borders.

The conception of a Bible commonwealth was already clear to them: they had entered into a covenant with God to erect a polity according to the pattern they conceived laid down in the New Testament, without the subsequent excrescences of history, without a hierarchy in church and state government. They did not at all question the hierarchy of social classes. This was the usual Elizabethan conception of society —except that they had no use for episcopacy, or for a nobility above them, or even, for that matter, of a monarchy, since Christ was their king. I think we may say that there was an incipient republicanism

in Massachusetts from the beginning. As for the hierarchical organization of society, they were not keen to recognize any order above themselves, though quite clear that there were people below them. It is a very middle-class point of view, and the Puritans were essentially middle-class.

To achieve the ends of this Bible commonwealth they had entered into a covenant with each other: "We have professed to enterprise these actions upon these and these ends . . . We must be knit together in this work as one man, we must entertain each other in brotherly affection." They were embarked upon a mission, "for we must consider that we shall be as a city upon a hill, the eyes of all people are upon us." If they failed in their endeavor, God would make them "a story and a by-word through the world, we shall open the mouths of enemies to speak evil of the ways of God and all professors for God's sake." On the other hand, if they succeeded, men would say of

In 1620, before leaving Holland in the Speedwell, *the Pilgrims prayed in the Reformed Church at Delfshaven (above).*

50

later settlements, "the Lord make it like that of New England." We recognize thus early that exemplary element, so different from other colonies, the sense of mission that is so strong in the American make-up today. That came from the Bay Puritans, not from the Plymouth Pilgrims.

The cornerstone of all their churches was a covenant. We find it clearly stated by one of their mentors, the Elizabethan Henry Jacob, a generation before: "A free mutual consent of believers joining and covenanting to live as members of a holy society together in all religious and virtuous duties as Christ and his apostles did institute and practice in the Gospel." Upon this they were all agreed, with their religious experience in the Old World, whether in England or Holland, behind them.

Actually while John Cotton was minister of the parish church of Boston in Lincolnshire, he entered into a covenant with some members of his congregation. It is not surprising that during his pastorate, though apparently not by his responsibility, the Puritans defaced the sculpture and monuments and broke all the stained glass in that splendid church—so that two or three centuries later the Victorians had to be at the pains of replacing it all with glass much less good.

It was this cornerstone of a congregational covenant that made them Congregationalists. The Pilgrims at Plymouth were rather a different case, though it seems to be questioned today whether they were absolutely Separatists, wishing to be regarded as utterly separated from the Church of England. Their mentor John Robinson at Leyden rather changed his position about this, and came back to the idea of being still members of the Church, agreeing in Christian beliefs, though not in Church government. And though the enemies of the Pilgrims called them Brownists— Robert Browne had been very vituperative about the Elizabethan bishops—in fact the Plymouth Pilgrims did not descend from Browne: they had an independent ancestry of their own in the Scrooby congregation, and its pastors and mentors, John Smyth, Richard Clifton, John Robinson, Elder Brewster. As for the vastly more important Massachusetts Puritans, they held themselves to be Puritan congregations of the Church of England and regarded separation as a sin. They were out to set a better model, away from the corruptions of the Old World, and by their example to convert the Church at home, upon which they had their eyes fixed.

As the *Talbot* drew away from Land's End in 1629 —a part of the Puritans' first plantation fleet, largest that had ever set sail for New England—Francis Higginson gathered the passengers in the stern to take their last sight of England. He spoke these words:

We will not say as the Separatists were wont to say at their leaving of England, Farewell Babylon! Farewell Rome! But we will say, Farewell dear England! Farewell the Church of God in England, and all the Christian friends there! We do not go to New England as Separatists from the Church of England, though we cannot but separate from the corruptions in it: but we go to practice the positive part of Church Reformation, and propagate the gospel in America.

e have already seen that there was this difference between the Plymouth people and the Bay Colony: that the Pilgrims were self-effacing exiles who only wanted to escape attention to worship and live in their own way; the Massachusetts Puritans were a governing body going forth to convert others to their way and impose it on others, so far as they could.

The nineteenth century immensely exaggerated the importance of the Pilgrim Fathers. Their story was told in countless books and then put into verse by Longfellow. To judge from its literature anyone would think that America started with them, and I wonder whether that is not the popular belief still. But this series of articles has shown to what diverse sources the nation goes back, way beyond Jamestown

Only known portrait of a Pilgrim in America is that of Edward Winslow, one of the governors of Plymouth Colony.

51

in the generation before the Plymouth Colony, to two generations earlier—the 1580's, high watermark of the Elizabethan Age, when everything begins together, including the colonization of America, to prove in the fullness of time the grandest achievement of the age.

It seems to bother American historians that New England did not come up to modern democratic standards. In their disappointment they have failed to observe what an advance all the colonies made in this respect on the Elizabethan England they came out of. The Pilgrims had the advantage of priority, and thereby exerted an influence by the example they set of civil marriage and in the registering of deeds. Theirs also was the first Congregational church, a working model already in being when the Massachusetts Puritans began to arrive.

But in every other respect the influence was all the other way. The size, power, and importance of the Bay Colony began to tell, until ultimately it absorbed Plymouth.

The religion, and thereby the mentality, of New England was entirely English in its sources, in spite of the Pilgrims' sojourn in Holland. The Scrooby flock settled at Leyden, where John Robinson was publicly ordained as their pastor; Brewster became their ruling elder. In the discussions prior to emigration it was agreed that if a majority of the congregation volunteered, Robinson should go as their pastor. To his disappointment only a minority volunteered. Only thirty-seven of the hundred or more passengers on board the *Mayflower* were Pilgrims from Leyden; we do not know who the rest were, but some of them we learn from Bradford were profane fellows.

Robinson remained behind to minister to the majority; after his death further groups from his congregation did go to New England. Meanwhile he refused to sanction the administration of the sacraments by Elder Brewster at Plymouth: not being ordained, Brewster might preach and pray, but not give communion to the flock. Robinson kept hoping that he might be able to join them; he sent them spiritual advice and consolation, but he was removed shortly to a better world. The state of the Pilgrims at Plymouth may be described as one of "Waiting for Robinson."

However, they seem to have got on very well without him. Elder Brewster, a mature man of fifty-three when they landed at Plymouth, had already had a wide and varied experience. He had been for a short time at Peterhouse, Cambridge, where he acquired nonconforming ideas. In 1590 he succeeded his father as postmaster at Scrooby, where he remained as pillar of the congregation till 1608. "After some investigation of their proceedings by the High Commission at York," says the *Dictionary of American Biography*, "which certainly did not amount to persecution, they decided to leave so ungodly a land." They found Amsterdam uncongenial, so they went on to Leyden; when they found Leyden not altogether congenial, only the wilderness would do. To the wilderness they went.

Social life in Plymouth has been described as "undoubtedly quiet in the extreme"; but Brewster, according to Bradford, was "of a very cheerful spirit, very sociable and pleasant amongst his friends." He had an excellent library of some four hundred books,

CONTINUED ON PAGE 78

Plymouth Colony owed most to the "benevolent autocracy" of William Bradford, who was born in Austerfield, Yorkshire, and was baptised in St. Helena's Church (left). A cradle of New England was St. Botolph's in Boston, Lincolnshire (right), the parish church of John Cotton; from Boston came five future governors of Massachusetts.

The Ultimate Courage

Few among the foreign missionaries to the

North American Indians surpassed him in

nobility; none was more cruelly martyred.

By ROBERT L. REYNOLDS

In both stature and spirit Jean de Brébeuf was a giant of a man; a superior called him "the Ajax of the mission."

Until the Allied landings in Normandy there stood on the edge of the village of Condé-sur-Vire, seven miles from Saint-Lô, two ancient and deserted buildings, stoutly fashioned of native stone. The larger of the two seemed to have been used as a barn, or perhaps as a chapel; in the other, according to an old and persistent legend, there was born on March 25, 1593, a child named Jean de Brébeuf, who was to bring to his native village, to Normandy, and to France itself a glory that almost four centuries have failed to efface.

His ancestors, an "ancient and a noble family" of landowners, had crossed the Channel with William the Conqueror and followed the banners of Louis IX to the Holy Land. Jean's personal crusade was to be of another nature: clad not in mail but in the black cassock and round flat hat of the Society of Jesus, he was to spend his strength and zeal in faraway Canada, working for the salvation of an obscure tribe of Indians. In that effort he would labor for many heartbreaking years with little success. In the process he would lose his life, after excruciating tortures. But in the end he would win what was to him a higher goal: martyrdom and canonization as a saint of the Catholic Church. And he would have an honored place in a story which for pure heroism is virtually without parallel in modern history—the effort of the Jesuits over a century and a half to convert and civilize the savages of New France.

De Brébeuf and the Jesuits came to Canada on the crest of a spiritual renewal that was sweeping France in the seventeenth century. It was the springtime of Catholicism's Counter Reformation, and the Jesuits themselves were sending missionaries to the farthest ends of the earth: to China and Japan, to Africa and South America. In France, despite a vocal Protestant minority, the colleges run by the Society were rapidly increasing in number and were becoming the popular schools of the time; in one of these, newly opened in Caen, not far from his birthplace, young Jean de Brébeuf enrolled at the age of sixteen. When the college was forced to close a year later—for a third of Normandy was Huguenot, and the Jesuits were bitterly opposed—he continued privately under his former masters and in 1617 presented himself at their novitiate at Rouen to study for the priesthood. At twenty-four he was, says his biographer, Francis X. Talbot,

# of Jean de Brébeuf

exceptionally tall, more than a head higher than the average Norman; he was somewhat lean, but broad-shouldered and well-built; his head was oblong, rather tapering at the top; the features were pronouncedly Norman, with prominent nose, generous lips, high cheekbones, and good eyes, that looked steadily and unafraid; his bearing, it seemed to the Master of Novices, was that of an old-time Norman knight.

From childhood he had heard of Canada, for it seems that Norman fishermen had been going to the Newfoundland banks since before Columbus' first voyage. A few decades later, in 1527, an English ship captain looking for a northwest passage had dropped anchor off what is now St. John's and had reported that he saw there "eleven saile of Normans, and one Brittaine, and two Portugall barkes, and all a-fishing." Two Jesuit priests had gone to Port Royal, France's first settlement in North America, in 1611; at home, Jean de Brébeuf read eagerly of their missionary experiences. So it was not remarkable that when, in the fall of 1624, two years after his ordination, he met and talked with two Franciscan missionaries who had just returned from New France, everything in his experience—his family background, his Norman ancestry, the spiritual ferment of the time, and his own developing zeal—should have led de Brébeuf to volunteer for service there.

The Franciscans—called Récollets because their rule of life stressed meditation—had been brought over by Champlain in 1615. But they were poor, and they were not very numerous. Moreover, they had been the victims of political intrigue on the part of those controlling the colony. The Récollets rightly assumed that the Jesuits had the manpower, the material resources, and the influence at court to overcome these handicaps to successful missionary endeavor; the two orders united their appeals to the Duc de Ventadour, Viceroy of New France, and in March, 1625, the Jesuits were officially empowered to join their Franciscan brethren in Canada.

A month later Father de Brébeuf, with four other Jesuits, took ship at Dieppe and after a voyage of nearly two months sailed up the broad St. Lawrence—"beautiful as the Seine, rapid as the Rhone, and deep as the sea," Champlain had called it—and caught his first glimpse of the high rock of Quebec.

The town, which was to serve as his base of operations, was in 1625 a miserable, scraggly little settlement

that almost any adverse circumstance—an epidemic, an unusually severe winter, an Indian attack—could have erased with ease. Though Cartier had planted the fleur-de-lis there almost a century before, and though the able Champlain had solidified the claim in 1608, all of New France still had only fifty-one year-round residents, two-thirds of them fur traders who spent most of their time with the Indians. Almost the only buildings in Quebec were Champlain's residence, a warehouse, and a few rude shacks. Two decades earlier, at Port Royal, a young lawyer named Marc Lescarbot had accurately set forth the conditions for successful colonization in a distant land. "Farming must be our goal," he had written, ". . . for whoso has corn, wine, cattle, linen, cloth, leather, iron, and lastly codfish, need have nought to do with treasure." But few peasants or artisans followed the flag westward; not until 1663, when the all-powerful Louis XIV turned his eyes toward New France, would it receive enough colonists to give it viability. Meanwhile, it remained in the hands of a succession of mercenary fur-trading companies which opposed colonization as endangering their monopoly of the country. They also conspired against the missionaries, who threatened their trade by opposing the sale of rum to the Indians and by trying to get the wandering tribes to abandon trapping and settle down, the better to plant the seeds of civilization and Christianity among them.

With one of these tribes, the Montagnais, who occupied the country around Quebec, de Brébeuf spent his first autumn and winter in Canada. They were a shiftless, nomadic people who hunted and fished for their subsistence and never laid anything by against a lean season. Even Brother Gabriel Sagard, the sympathetic Récollet who had observed them two years before, dubbed them "the rabble of the forest." Now, trekking

TEXT CONTINUED ON PAGE 58

OVERLEAF: This engraving of 1664 shows the martyrdom of several Jesuits and their lay assistants in New France, which occurred at various times and places, as if they had happened simultaneously. De Brébeuf (6) and Gabriel Lalemant (7) were put to death by the Iroquois near what is now Midland, Ontario, on March 16 and 17, 1649. Seventeen months earlier Isaac Jogues (2), who had worked with de Brébeuf among the Hurons, had been tomahawked in a Mohawk village near present-day Auriesville, New York.

Preciosa mors quorundam Patrum é Societ. Iesu in noua Francia. I. P. Annas Denoüe Campanus, Caritatis officia exercens, frigore enecatur. 2. Febr. 1646. 2. ϛ. P. Anton. Daniel Deppensis, gregi suo Vitam seruare volens, interficitur. 4. Iul. 1648. 6. 7. P. Ioa. de Brebeuf diœc. Baiocens. et P. Gabriel Lallemant parisin. 16. et 17. mart 1649. 8. P. Carol. Garnier parisinus Pastoris officio fungens, sclopis impetitur. 7. Decemb. 1649. 9. P. Natal. chabanel diœc. Mimatens. ab apostata.

Greg. Huret f.

ques Aurelianus, christum ad Hiroquæos portans, Dæmonem attulisse creditus; ... ri percussus ... de 1647. 3 ... uenes ... ...omites trucidata ...candentibusque igni securibus ad collum appensis, exusti aquâ ebullienti in Baptism... ... er ...ua ... ...or aliiq; Caraibus inter ... ...mpis in profluentem dejectus est. 10 Ioseph Onahare iuuenis Algonquinus a christi laudibus ce ... ...ibus dictis les demoqu ... ...ur ann. ...

The "Island of Birds," in the mouth of the St. Lawrence, as one Jesuit priest saw it.

with them through the countryside, sweltering on the warm, sunny autumn days and freezing as snow began to blanket the hills; sharing their feasts when game was plentiful and their hunger when it was not, Jean de Brébeuf found within himself the indispensable gift of every successful missionary: adaptability.

The child of a sophisticated culture, he was still able to conceal his disgust when at mealtime all dipped their hands into the common pot and afterward wiped them on their hair. He was sworn to celibacy, and yet as he warded off the advances of the promiscuous Indian girls he managed to avoid giving offence. He was honestly curious about their customs, social as well as religious. But his most useful talent was his ability to learn their language.

The dialects of the Canadian tribes were not easy; years later the intelligent Mère Marie de l'Incarnation, setting up in Quebec an Ursuline school for Indian girls, would complain that the words rattled around in her head like stones. Yet in those few months with the Montagnais Father de Brébeuf not only learned to converse fluently with his hosts, but compiled a Montagnais dictionary and started writing a grammar.

These were almost the only tangible fruits of that first fall and winter, but de Brébeuf did not consider that the time had been wasted. He had had a valuable introduction to Indian ways and was inwardly reassured by the fact that he himself had passed a difficult test. It would be good preparation for his work among the Indians of another tribe on which he and the rest

of the Jesuit missionaries had already set their sights.

These were the proud and intelligent Hurons—"the nobility of the forest," in Sagard's Indian hierarchy—who inhabited the shores of Lake Huron, far to the west of Quebec. There were several reasons why the Jesuits preferred to concentrate their missionary efforts there rather than among the more available Montagnais. For one thing, the Hurons lived a relatively settled existence, and thus it would be easier to establish lasting missions among them. For another, the Récollets had already spent some time in the Huron country; priests were not total strangers there. And finally, Huronia was strategically located at the center of the vast network of rivers and lakes that controlled the heart of the continent; success there might open the way to similar conversions among the tribes to the north, south, and west.

As the brief spring days of the year 1626 lengthened into summer, Father de Brébeuf awaited the arrival of the Huron canoes, which annually made their way down to the French settlements to trade. When they came in July he managed, by dint of many presents, to secure a place between two dusky paddlers before the flotilla headed for home. With him, in other canoes, went the Récollet Joseph de la Roche Daillon and another Jesuit, Father Anne de Noüe. As de Brébeuf folded his tall frame into the narrow birch-bark boat, the great Huron mission, perhaps the most intensive evangelizing effort ever launched among a single North American tribe, had begun. What it would cost over the next twenty-five years in tears and blood would be known, finally, only to the priests who shed them.

Everything about the mission to the Hurons was difficult, beginning with the route to their country. The returning canoes headed southwestward along the St. Lawrence, passed the mouth of the Richelieu, which flows north from Lake Champlain, and turned into the Rivière des Prairies near the present site of Montreal. Having crossed the Lake of Two Mountains, they finally entered the muddy, boiling Ottawa River, and watched the days stretch into weeks as they followed it north and west. Altogether, as they fought their way against the current, de Brébeuf—pressed into service as a paddler now—counted thirty-five portages; in addition, he and his Indian companions were forced more than fifty times to get out and wade through the swift and angry waters, pushing or dragging their boats as they went. They paddled all day without rest. At night, after a tasteless meal of *sagamité*—boiled, unsalted corn mush—they lay down to sleep on the forest floor, de Brébeuf nodding over his breviary by firelight before joining the others in an exhausted slumber.

Arrived in the upper reaches of the Ottawa, they

paused for a day or two among the friendly Nipissings, who lived near the placid lake named for their tribe, then dropped down along French River until they finally reached Lake Huron, called by Champlain the Freshwater Sea. They headed south and east then, advancing the stroke as they neared the end of their journey, and at last beached their canoes on the southeast shore of what is now Georgian Bay, near Midland, in Simcoe County, Ontario. After thirty days and a thousand miles of paddling and portaging, the Hurons were home.

How the three priests survived the long, wearing journey may be read between the lines of a set of instructions de Brébeuf later wrote for the Jesuits who would follow him:

To conciliate the Savages, you must be careful never to make them wait for you in embarking. You must provide yourself with a tinder box or with a burning mirror, or with both, to furnish them fire in the daytime to light their pipes, and in the evening when they have to encamp; these little services win their hearts. You should try to eat their sagamité or salmagundi in the way they prepare it, although it may be dirty, half-cooked, and very tasteless. . . .
You must be prompt in embarking and disembarking; and tuck up your gowns so that they will not get wet, and so that you will not carry either water or sand into the canoe. . . . Be careful not to annoy anyone in the canoe with your hat; it would be better to take your nightcap. There is no impropriety among the Savages. . . .

De Brébeuf himself must have observed these precautions carefully, for the two braves whose boat he had shared gave a good report of him to their chiefs, and he was well received in their villages.

Within a few weeks de la Roche Daillon left to establish contact with the Tobacco Nation to the west and the Neutral Nation to the south. De Brébeuf and de Noüe, however, remained among the Hurons. These people called themselves Ouendats; "Huron" was a French appellation after the ridge of hair which some of the men wore from nape to brow, giving their heads the look of a *hure*, or boar's head. De Brébeuf estimated that they numbered some 30,000 souls, in about twenty villages between Georgian Bay and Lake Simcoe to the southeast. The country was wooded and hilly, but with many broad and well-watered meadows on which such crops as wheat and peas grew wild. In the main the Hurons were a sedentary people who lived by trade and agriculture. They raised beans, pumpkins, tobacco, and some fruits, but their principal crop was corn, from which they made their *sagamité*. This, supplemented occasionally by a bit of fish or game and served in a wooden bowl "broad as an alms dish," was their "soup, meat, and dessert of every day."

When the French first came to their country the Hurons were a stone-age people whose primitive farming methods periodically exhausted the land, forcing them to move their villages every fifteen years. Yet these villages were surprisingly well constructed, and those on the east and south, nearest the country of their traditional enemies, the Iroquois, were strongly palisaded. Their houses were long, domed lodges built of saplings covered with bark. A wide aisle ran down the middle, and on either side of this a sleeping shelf was built four or five feet off the ground. The only ventilation was a slit in the roof to let out the smoke of the cooking fires. Such a lodge, which might be over two hundred feet long by about thirty wide, was shared by more than twenty families.

The Huron way of life gave the lie to the notion, which nevertheless persisted in Europe, that the Indian uncontaminated by white civilization lived a spartan existence marked by orderly habits and natural virtue. De Brébeuf seems from the first to have conceived an affection for the Hurons quite unrelated to the fact that they were targets for conversion. Yet this did not blind him to their faults: they were dirty, and so lazy that the men did little work not forced upon them by necessity. Also, they were inveterate gamblers. One of their principal games made use of a large wooden bowl into which the player put five or six fruit stones or flattened balls colored black on one side and white or yellow on the other. These were rolled out like dice, and on the turn of the stones the

CONTINUED ON PAGE 102

FROM *Historiae Canadensis*

Indian costume: "Hurons think it beautiful to have . . . prominent lips and narrow eyes."

The remarkable document here printed for the first time doubtless offers the last full ray of light that will be thrown on the events of the night Lincoln was assassinated. The conspirators' attempt on the life of Secretary Seward is now described, with astonishing minuteness and vividness, in the diary of his daughter.—*Allan Nevins*

"*I have supped full on horrors*"

Fanny Seward, who hoped for literary fame,

left a chilling account—hitherto unpublished—

of the hideous evening which blighted her life

Edited and with an introduction by PATRICIA CARLEY JOHNSON

The portrait of Frances Adeline Seward, opposite, painted by Emanuel Leutze a year after her death at twenty-one, now hangs in the Seward House in Auburn, New York. Her diary (right) is in the collection of her father's papers at the University of Rochester library.

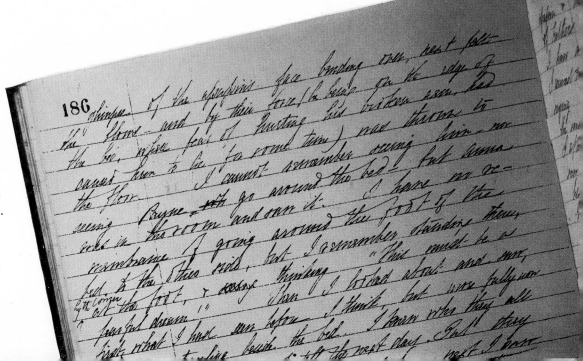

THE
SEWARDS

William Henry Seward, Jr.

Augustus Seward

Anna Wharton Seward

Frederick William Seward

With Mrs. Seward absent from Washington, the role of official hostess for the Seward household fell to Anna, wife of Seward's second son and Assistant Secretary of State, Frederick. The eldest son, Augustus, shared his mother's dislike of "society," and his visits home, from duty with the Regular Army in the West, were infrequent. Fanny's favorite, because he had been her childhood companion, was Seward's namesake, William Henry, Jr., a tall man with dark curling hair.

Frances Adeline Seward (called Fanny to distinguish her from her mother, for whom she was named) wanted to be a writer. To this end, for literary practice, she began Christmas Day, 1858, shortly after her fourteenth birthday, to keep a diary. The last entry was made October 7, 1866, three weeks before her death. The result is one of the most sensitive, poignant, and sometimes amusing manuscripts to come from the Civil War period. It reveals more than the aspirations of an intelligent young woman to break the bonds of Victorianism and at the same time not to be classed "a blue stocking." It presents a frank view of social Washington, with its constant round of calls, weekly reception days, and gala balls that were often more like work than pleasure for a statesman's family; and an intimate one of a family regarded by contemporaries as an ideal of mutual tenderness, consideration, and affection.

One of the major problems for the Sewards was that despite their sincere attachment to each other they were rarely together. Mrs. Seward had suffered for more than twenty years from recurring attacks of neuralgia, which prostrated her for days and sometimes weeks. Excitement or fatigue brought her either a headache or a mild heart murmur. And nothing fatigued her more quickly than the duties of a politician's wife. She detested the rigidity of Washington protocol, the oceans of cards to be acknowledged, and the fact that every pleasant day had to be devoted to calls. As her health continued to decline, she retired to the quiet of the family home in Auburn, New York.

Thus it was, in a family as divided by circumstance as the country was by war, that Fanny Seward grew to young womanhood. She "came out" in Washington society at the Secretary's annual New Year's Day reception in 1863, but she was not considered a "belle." Her features were too heavy for the Victorian ideal of beauty, and her hair, though long and thick, was Indian-straight and a common shade of brown. Her luminous dark eyes, however, contrasted attractively with a pale, clear complexion. She was unfashionably tall, and aware of it. She often felt herself "awkward, stale and unprofitable." Though trained by private tutors in the social graces of music, painting, horseback riding, and French, her achievements in these fields were never more than fair. She couldn't dance more than a simple quadrille, and she never had a beau nor seemingly any desire for one.

Yet constant association with adults matured her quickly. She gradually overcame her shyness to the point where she could preside gracefully as hostess at formal dinners and at the weekly Wednesday receptions. If conversation turned to books or the theater, Fanny waxed enthusiastic and knowledgeable. She conversed intelligently about Dickens, Thackeray, Ruskin, Longfellow, Whittier, or the current Northern literary rage, Theodore Winthrop. She was an avid theater-goer and confided to her diary rapt accounts of such stars as Edward Davenport, James Murdoch, Edwin Forrest; the Sewards' close personal friend, Charlotte Cushman; and John Wilkes Booth's brother Edwin, who came to dine with the Sewards the evening he played *Hamlet* in Washington during March, 1864. She thought him a "sad, sensitive, dignified gentleman."

Fanny formed very strong opinions and her descriptions of prominent people were not always flattering. Although she liked two of Lincoln's private secretaries, John Nicolay and John Hay, she characterized the third, William Stoddard, "as excessively ill-looking, conceited and disagreeable; very flat & silly in conversation, and grins abominably." Novelist Anthony Trollope was "a great homely, red, stupid faced Englishman, with a disgusting beard." The wives of Senators John Crittenden and Ira Harris appear as "two very fat bundles of hair, feathers, lace & jewelry—who grew dreadfully uninteresting."

For all her youth and occasional high spirits there was a certain melancholy about Fanny Seward. Perhaps she realized that she was gradually losing her patient struggle with ill health. Since a childhood bout with typhoid fever she had been subject to severe chills, fevers, and a nagging cough which she predicted would eventually "carry me off."

When tragedy finally struck the Sewards it took a dreadful toll. Fanny's account of what she witnessed on Assassination Night, 1865, is printed here just as she wrote it—with her punctuation and misspellings preserved—but she could not record the final results. Major Augustus Seward's wounds proved superficial. The Secretary of State also recovered. But when he resumed his post, friends and foes alike were shocked by his aged, infirm appearance and the jagged marks that twisted the right side of his face. Frederick, suffering a fracture of the skull, lay unconscious for weeks and throughout his life wore a skull cap to hide his scars. Yet he was eighty-five when he died, in 1915.

Gradually the horror faded and a deeper sorrow took its place. Oppressed by anxiety and suffering from shock, Mrs. Seward's frail health collapsed and she died two months after the assassination attempt. Grief over the loss of her mother, constant fear for her father and brother, combined with sleepless nights, hastily eaten meals, and overwork, undermined Fanny's limited resources. She spent the next year patiently enduring the steadily worsening cough which indeed "carried her off" on October 29, 1866.

—*Patricia Carley Johnson*

Secretary of State William H. Seward, as the Civil War ended, could well regard himself as one of the architects of victory. Sagacity, firmness, and cautious foresight had marked his course. By his stern front he had taught the British and French governments to respect this country, intimidated foreign interventionists, and checkmated at every point the Confederate agents abroad. "Our foreign relations," he wrote his family just before Appomattox, "are closing up finely."

Leslie's Illustrated, MAY 20, 1865

The Seward house on Lafayette Square.

What we may call the Victory Fortnight of the North had begun April 1, 1865, when President Lincoln, who was visiting General Grant's headquarters at City Point, learned that Phil Sheridan had captured Five Forks, and thus severed the railroad which was Robert E. Lee's lifeline with Danville and the South. While Lincoln was at City Point, Secretary of State William H. Seward looked after routine Administration matters. No member of the Cabinet deserved more gratitude. Long the most unpopular figure of the Administration, so bitterly hated by Radical Republicans that at the end of 1862 they had almost ousted him from the government, he had gradually won the respect he deserved.

On April 5 Seward telegraphed the President that some papers, important but not critical, required attention, and that he would bring them down if Lincoln wished to tarry on the James. But Lincoln replied that he would be back within two days. Actually he was delayed, and it was not until the ninth that his boat, the River Queen, *chugged from the Chesapeake up the Potomac, a journey he relieved by reading Shakespeare aloud. Meanwhile Seward suffered the first of the calamities described by his daughter.—Ed.*

Payne mounts the stairs in the Seward home.

CULVER SERVICE

*W*ednsday April 5ᵗʰ   I went in the afternoon to make a call, met Father in the Dept wagon. Anna was not well—had been ailing several days. She took a little drive with us. After that Mary Titus [1] and I went to the Dept. for Father and Fred—stopped at our door for Father's coat, drove out Vermount Avenue. The carriage door not being tightly closed kept flying open. The coachman was told to dismount & shut it. While he was doing so the horses started. The coachman, (Henry Key) had the reins in his hand, and was swung by them some distance. Fred immediately jumped out, thinking to head the horses. Although they were not going very fast he was thrown to the ground. The horses turned round with a rapid sweep & went on increasing their speed. Father had some idea of being able to stop them, & sprang from the carriage in spite of my entreaties that he would not jump. I was on the back seat & could not see whether he reached the ground safely or not. Mary was opposite me. The horses tore along. I had a momentary thought of catching the reins, but they were swinging widely in the air far beyond my reach. We passed the Wilkes' [2]— I saw the houses & the sidewalk lit with peaceful sunshine while we seemed to be whirling on to certain destruction. At the alley between Mʳ Tayloe's [3] house & ours the horses turned. We brushed against a tree. The brick corner of the house was in front—I was sure we were to be dashed against it and crushed to death. But just there the off horse fell, all crowded in between his mate and the carriage. Before we had time to get out of the carriage, the horse was up again, & we were dashing down the alley, when a soldier headed & stopped the horses, & saved us from being dragged into the stable. As soon as we could get out I hastened back to look for Father, I met a crowd of men carrying him, & I thought he was dead, but they told me no. Then Fred came up. He sent me to tell Anna to prepare a bed. While I stood in our hall the men carried Father in & up stairs. A rough man told me Father was not hurt, only his nose was cut—(he was bleeding) Anna went up stairs. I rested in the library then went to my own room—Anna came in two or three times— Said Father was insensible & would not know me. The doctors were there. He came gradually to conciousness, was bewildered at first. One of the surgeons examined his arm—I could hear the cries which the pain of the examination caused him. The right arm was found broken between the shoulder and the elbow. About six o'c. Anna came and told me Father would know me

[1] An intimate friend and contemporary of Fanny's from Auburn.
[2] Home of Admiral Charles Wilkes on H Street.
[3] Benjamin Ogle Tayloe, one of a group of distinguished old-time residents of Washington.

now. I went into the room—he was so disfigured by bruises, his face so swollen, that he had scarcely a trace of resemblance to himself. His eyes were closed by immense swellings. Anna told him I was there, and he said. "And you were not hurt?" "No." "And Mary was not hurt?" "No." Mr Gutman [4] was there— Presently I was bidden to go down to dinner—Gus & I while the rest waited with Father. I found Mr Stanton in the hall below. When I came up a few minutes after he was siting by Father's bed-side. Anna told me to apply a wash once in 15 min. to Father's face. The blood from his nose was almost suffocating him— Gus wiped it away. Mr Stanton wiped his lips—spoke gently to him—and was like a woman in the sickroom—& much more efficient than I, who did not know what to do.

Many kind friends called to offer their services, or enquire. Fred told me that when he had got up from his own fall he ran & found Father lying on the ground, his great, heavy overcoat over his head, in a stifling way. Fosburg [5] found the heel off one of the shoes he wore, a new pair, which showed that he must have caught his heel in getting out, & that threw him on his face.

The Surgeon General, (Dr Barnes,) Dr Norris (medical officer attending officers of Reg. Army here) and Dr Verdi [6] were here. The case was placed in the hands of the Surgeon General, & Dr Norris had special care.

Mother was telegraphed of the accident, & I wrote a few words home.

Thursday April 6th After breakfast I wrote a few lines to Mother, since we do not hear of her having left Auburn—& that others might open them if she had left. Mr Gutman, going to Pittsburg, to be married next Tuesday, came to take leave of us. Father's face is terribly swollen, & he bears no likeness to himself. I sat up till three o'clock in the morning— Father was restless, & talking constantly, in his sleep—holding my hand.

Friday April 7th Mother & Will came in the evening —the late train. Father had been expecting them. I told Mother before she saw father, something of his appearance—still she was much shocked by it. I had thought there was no danger in his situation, but she explained to me that of congestion & inflammation, which made me feel very badly. Retired late.

The diary from which I copy has this note "I have been so hurried that these pages are filled up long after their date, & I cannot give many particulars."

[4] A. Anthony Gutman, Seward's secretary at the State Department.

[5] Probably Gustav Forsberg, a Swedish steward employed by the family for over eight years.

[6] Dr. T. S. Verdi, the Seward family physician.

I remember meeting Mother at the foot of the stairs —& later, when she took a cup of tea in the dining room with Will, Fred was there, & when she asked about his broken arm, lifted a chair to show her that he had regained his strength. She had been sick on the way, but was looking well then—& was in the greatest anxiety about father when she came.

Saturday April 8th Father seemed better in the morning. The swelling of his face goes down. Dr Norris examined his jaw again today. (I think it was the day before that he first examined it—& discovered the fracture) It was in the morning. Fred, Anna & I were present— I never saw such agony —it was terrible to witness, & made me very sad. Fred sent Mr Patty to show Mary Titus some places of interest. Mother had a head-ache which kept her in her room most of the time. Clarence [7] was here in the evening— came in & saw father. It being Mary Titus' last night here I slept with her—retired at 12 o'c.

Sunday April 9th The swelling of father's face has subsided rapidly, making him look much more like himself. Secretary Stanton was here three times today. I shall never forget the scene this morning when Mr Stanton approached the bed, & father took his hand and in a strong voice cried, "God bless you Stanton—I can never tell you half——" "Don't try to speak, said Mr Stanton, whose face I could not see, but from his voice I judged him much affected— "You have made

CULVER SERVICE

Assassin Lewis Powell (alias Payne).

me cry for the first time in my life I believe," said Father. In the afternoon—Mr Stanton brought him fruit sent by Mrs Stanton. Clarence was here in the morning—& sat some time in Mother's room—she not being well was lying down. Clarence stayed to dinner— Mother's neuralgia was better. Will left for Auburn at

CONTINUED ON PAGE 96

[7] Clarence A. Seward, Fanny's cousin. While Seward and Fred were incapacitated from the assassination attempt he served as acting Assistant Secretary of State (April to August, 1865).

The Union gunboat looked like a clumsy turtle, but her

gallant dash past Island No. 10 helped divide the Confederacy

The CARONDELET
Runs the Gantlet

By PHILLIPS MELVILLE

The Carondelet *was built in 1861 at a pace interrupted by "neither the sanctity of the Sabbath nor the darkness of night."*

On the morning of March 15, 1862, the iron-clad gunboat *Carondelet*—Commander Henry Walke, U.S.N.—lay moored to the left bank of the Mississippi close to the Kentucky-Tennessee line. The river was up, swollen by spring rains and melted western snows, and the gunboat tugged uneasily at the web of lines that tethered her to the sparse cottonwoods as the yellow flood, dotted with debris and wreckage, slid relentlessly by.

Despite her musical name, the *Carondelet* could lay small claim to beauty except in a functional sense. To the eye of a deep-water navy man, accustomed to graceful sheer and lofty rigging, she must have resembled a prehistoric river monster more than a warship. Nor would he have been entirely mistaken. The ironclads were, in fact, creatures of the river, born on its banks, six of them on the outskirts of St. Louis, the remaining three at Mound City, Illinois.

In August of 1861, the quartermaster general had awarded the contract for their construction to James B. Eads, a prominent St. Louis engineer, who with phenomenal organizing skill and energy had driven 4,000 men night and day, seven days a week, to produce them in just one hundred days. He had contracted to do it in sixty-five days, but the government failed to live up to its agreement to make regular payments for the men's wages. There were unavoidable delays, and Eads was compelled to use his own funds, plus what he could borrow from patriotic friends, to get the job done. By the spring of '62 Eads had not yet been paid, and the ironclads fought their early battles more or less as private warships on loan to the government. Because they had been procured by the War Department they "belonged" to the Army, but they were manned and operated by the Navy, under Army directions. The arrangement did not work well, and would have been impossible had the flag-officer in command and the generals with whom he had to deal been men of small character.

Contemporary photographs reveal the appearance of the ironclads, but their construction and characteristics require some description. On a shallow-draft rectangular hull 175 feet long by about 50 feet wide were mounted five cylindrical boilers which drove two high-pressure engines, each connected to one end of a massive paddle wheel 22 feet in diameter. A box-like structure enclosed everything, including the paddle wheel. All four sides of this superstructure, or "casemate," sloped inward and upward from the water line at 35 degrees to deflect shot fired at close range. The casemate's forward face was armored with $2\frac{1}{2}$ inches of iron plate backed by 20 inches of solid oak. Opposite the boilers and engines the sides were similarly protected, but elsewhere were covered merely by heavy planking, as was the stern.* Considerations of weight and a specified maximum draft of 6 feet precluded additional armor except for some light shielding around the conical pilothouse. Forward, the casemate was pierced for three guns, on each side for four, and at the stern for two. The intended armament had been three 8-inch 64-pounder Dahlgrens; six 32-pounder smoothbores; and four 42-pounder army rifles; but variations existed among the ironclads due to the limited availability of guns. The designed speed of the boats was nine miles an hour, though actually they were seldom able to make more than six or seven. But despite their lack of speed and incomplete armor, they were far more formidable than any of the river gunboats possessed by the Confederates, and reflected great credit on their designer, Samuel M. Pook (better known as a creator of record-breaking clipper ships), in whose honor they were sometimes referred to as "Pook's turtles."

The *Carondelet* had six identical sister ships—*St. Louis, Pittsburgh, Cincinnati, Louisville, Cairo,* and *Mound City.* Because the seven were as alike as peas they were identified by individually colored bands about their twin stacks. The two remaining ironclads of the western flotilla—*Essex* and *Benton*—were larger. The *Benton* was a giant—187 feet long by 75 feet wide—mounting sixteen guns; she was selected as flagship for the flotilla by its commander, Flag-Officer Andrew H. Foote, U.S.N.

The *Carondelet* had already seen some hot action at the capture of Forts Henry and Donelson in February. At Donelson, on the Cumberland, Foote had led his gunboats up the river to within point-blank range of the Confederate guns. As a result they had taken a severe pounding that shortly sent two of them back down again, out of control, and a third limping out of the fight. The action taught Flag-Officer Foote and his gunboat skippers greater respect for Confederate guns and gunners and caused them to change their tactics when it came to attacking heavily defended positions.

The two closely related victories brought important strategic advantages. Besides opening the way for an advance into the heart of Tennessee, they compelled the evacuation of the Confederate stronghold at Columbus, Kentucky, with 140 guns and a garrison of 12,000, which had effectively closed the Mississippi against a southward advance.

* Popular belief to the contrary, neither the *Merrimac* nor her nemesis, the *Monitor,* was the first ironclad; indeed the European powers had tried out armored floating batteries a decade earlier. But the captured U.S. frigate *Merrimac,* which the Rebels converted into the *Virginia,* was the first American ship to be protected all around with iron. Her plating was four inches thick. [Ed.]

The crew of the Carondelet *was composed of young recruits, together with "enough men-o'-war's men to leaven the lump."*

The Confederates did not have to go far to find another spot suitable for a defense of the river. Sixty miles below Columbus at Island No. 10—so called because it was the tenth island below the mouth of the Ohio—they already had a fortified position of great natural strength. This they now proceeded to develop. (*See* map on page 71.)

At Island No. 10 the river makes a sudden northward turn of nearly 180 degrees, and here the Rebels had erected ten batteries, five of them on the island, the remainder on the Tennessee shore. About a mile above the bend was a redoubt containing six heavy guns. Because of the high water at this time the redoubt was partly flooded. Along the thirty-foot bluff rising above the bend the other four batteries were spaced a quarter-mile apart. Together the shore positions mounted twenty-four guns.

The emplacements on the island were all located along the north shore facing the Missouri swamps, for the main channel for river traffic lay on that side. The one at the head of the island was the largest, with seven guns; the other four, spaced at short intervals along the shore, mounted a total of thirteen. All of the island batteries stood from twenty to thirty feet above the river. A formidable reinforcement had been added in the form of a sixteen-gun floating battery moored against the island midway along its length.

There were no batteries on the Tennessee side of the island. There the channel was obstructed by snags at low water, though it may have been passable when the river was in flood. A single heavy battery was under construction at the tail of the island to cover the river in the direction of New Madrid, Missouri, seven miles below at the reverse bend. A large fortification was also being built on the mainland behind the island, as a protection against an attack from the rear, and to cover the landing place used by the fleet of light craft that shuttled between island and mainland. Guns in this work would also command the lower end of the Tennessee channel. Finally, to discourage any attempt to cross the river between Madrid Bend and Tiptonville, six miles south as the crow flies, twenty-one by water, batteries had been erected to cover each of the landing places.

Located on and about Island No. 10 were an estimated 7,000 Confederate troops, including several thousand in an entrenched camp at New Madrid. General John P. McCown, C.S.A., was in command until March 27, when he was relieved by General W. W. Mackall, former assistant adjutant general for Albert Sidney Johnston.

Immediately after the Union occupation of Columbus, Foote headed down the Mississippi toward Island No. 10 with the *Benton*, the *Carondelet* and five of her sister ironclads, ten mortar boats, and a small fleet of tugs and transports. At the same time a Union army of about 20,000 under Major General John Pope was working its way southward through the Missouri swamps toward New Madrid, which Pope proceeded to outflank by occupying Point Pleasant, on the western shore of the river, eight miles below. Thereupon the Confederate force encamped at New Madrid withdrew across the river, out of reach. Next day Pope occupied New Madrid and sat down to "estimate the situation."

He at once perceived that he was stalemated. So long as he was unable to cross the river the Confederates were secure, and because their light gunboats and batteries controlled the Mississippi below Island No. 10 there was little prospect that he could do so. In particular, he had no craft for mounting an amphibious assault, although there were plenty upriver. The solution would be to have Foote run a number of his ironclads down to New Madrid, drive off the Confederate mosquito fleet, and destroy the batteries at the landing places. The gunboats would then be available to ferry Pope's troops across the river. In this event the Confederates would be trapped, for the flood made impassable the semicircle of swamps, lakes, and bayous that separated the Tennessee shore from the hinterland. Nor, with Federal troops both upriver and down, could the Confederates make a withdrawal aboard the fleet of large steamers which they had moored behind Island No. 10. Surrender or capture was inevitable unless the river dropped and the swamps dried up, allowing escape by the back door.

At 9 A.M. on March 15, Foote and his flotilla arrived above Island No. 10. Leaving his transports and supply barges in the vicinity of Island No. 8 twelve miles above, he dropped down with the gunboats and mortars within range of the Confederate defenses. Within a few days he received a request from Pope that he run several of the ironclads past the island to New Madrid at the earliest practicable moment. Well informed as to the disposition and strength of the enemy's defenses, and remembering the hammering his gunboats had taken at less formidable Fort Donelson, Foote declined to send even one, convinced that the undertaking "would . . . result in the sacrifice of the boat, her officers and men, which sacrifice I should not be justified in making."

Instead, beginning on March 17, he attempted to reduce the Confederate stronghold by bombardment, hammering away at the Rebel batteries all day, every day. At times the Confederates had to scramble for their dugouts, but the damage was insignificant. Something very near a direct hit was necessary to destroy an enemy gun, for they were small and the range was nearly three miles. Defiantly, the large Confederate guns would lob a few shells upriver, with alarming accuracy. For the most part, however, the Rebels were content to save their ammunition so long as the ironclads kept their distance.

On March 20 Foote, under repeated urging by General Pope to send a gunboat down to New Madrid, instructed Commander Roger Stembel of the *Cincinnati* to sound out the other gunboat skippers, informally, regarding an attempt to run the gantlet. All of them said it was too risky—all, that is, except Commander Walke of the *Carondelet,* who said that it could and should be done. Foote was not yet ready to change his mind, however, and the bombardment dragged on until it had become a subject of ridicule in Pope's army. To the question, "What is the Navy doing today?" the standard reply was, "Oh, they're bombarding the State of Tennessee at long range, as usual."

On March 27, after ten days of steady but fruitless shelling, Pope was almost frantic with impatience, certain that the river must soon begin to fall and open an escape route for the Confederates through the swamps. He therefore composed a telegram to General Henry W. Halleck, his superior, who was showing signs of restlessness over Pope's long stay at New Madrid. "I will take Island No. 10 within a week. Trust me," it read. "As Commodore Foote is unable to reduce and unable to run his gunboats past it, I would ask, as they belong to the United States, that he be directed to remove the crews from two of them and turn the boats over to me. I will bring them here."

Halleck responded by wiring Foote to give Pope all possible assistance with the gunboats, but pointedly made no reference to turning them over to the Army. One wonders whether Pope really expected this drastic suggestion to be taken seriously; perhaps he hoped that some word of it would get to Foote and stir him to action. At any rate, within the next two days Foote took the step that was to lead to the *Carondelet*'s famous exploit.

He summoned the gunboat commanders to a coun-

Flag-Officer Foote, flotilla commander, would not order his boats past the island.

Commander Walke, skipper of the Carondelet, *insisted that the job could be done.*

cil of war aboard the *Benton.* As on the occasion of the informal interview with Stembel, all but one of the officers insisted that it was impracticable. Again Walke dissented, arguing that it could be done "under favorable circumstances" and that in any case it was the only way around the existing impasse. When Foote asked him if he would undertake the mission with the *Carondelet,* Walke said he would.

Foote replied that a great load of responsibility had been lifted from his shoulders. He would never, he said, have countenanced an attempt except on a volunteer basis. He promised to issue written orders immediately.

Walke received them in a letter of instruction on March 30. "You will avail yourself of the first fog or rainy night and drift your steamer down past . . . Island No. 10 until you reach New Madrid," the letter said. It concluded by commending Walke "to the care and protection of God," but evidently Foote doubted that the Almighty would favor the enterprise: he added a postscript giving instructions for destroying the *Carondelet* in the event of grounding and imminent capture.

Work was immediately begun to prepare the *Carondelet* for the ordeal. Planking from a damaged barge was used to cover the hurricane deck, and heavy chain was laid over it as a protection against plunging shot. Hawsers and chain cable were wound around the pilothouse to a depth of eleven to eighteen inches, and a stout barricade was erected about the boilers and engines. To silence the puffing of the exhaust steam as it discharged from the stacks while under way, the lines were disconnected and redirected into the paddle-wheel housing. Gradually, as Walke later wrote, the ironclad took on the appearance of "a farmer's wagon, prepared for market." Finally, arrangements were made to lash a barge, loaded with coal and piled with baled hay to a height that would cover the gun ports, alongside the unarmored portion of the casemate.

A few days before, two projects had been carried out with a view to improving the prospects for success. The first was a boldly conceived and executed "commando" raid on the Confederate redoubt, already slightly damaged by Foote's bombardment. On the night of April 1, Colonel George W. Roberts of the Forty-second Illinois Regiment, with fifty men in five boats, dropped silently down river, stormed ashore with fixed bayonets, and effectively spiked all six guns before making a leisurely withdrawal. The second project was the elimination of the floating battery: the mortar boats concentrated their fire on it, and reconnaissance the following morning disclosed it an-

chored about midstream three miles below the island.

By April 4 the preparations were complete. The day was humid and cloudy, and it appeared that conditions might be suitable for a run down that night. Commander Walke notified Foote that if they were, he would make the attempt at 10 P.M., by which time the moon would have gone down. First Master William R. Hoel of the *Cincinnati,* whose twenty-one years as a Mississippi pilot had made him familiar with every twist and turn of the river, now came aboard as acting master. His first move was to call a meeting of the pilots to discuss the problems of navigation.

An extensive sand bar extended from the apex of the Missouri peninsula out past mid-river. (*See* map opposite.) When the river was at normal stages, this compelled descending traffic to stand over toward the Tennessee shore and pass within close range of the batteries along the bluff. It was then necessary to turn abruptly to starboard in order to continue down the Missouri channel, thus coming within easy range of the guns on Island No. 10. During the passage a vessel would be subject to both a raking and a cross fire. As an alternative there was a narrow channel across the sand bar, navigable only at high water, that would allow a vessel to pass at longer range from the Tennessee batteries, but this passage was enfiladed throughout its length by the battery at the head of the island. An irregular though navigable "chute" existed close along the Missouri shore, but the Confederates had blocked it by sinking a steamer in its lower end. The decision was to go down the Missouri channel.

Conditions were still favorable as darkness approached. Commander Walke assembled his crew and passengers—among the latter a volunteer detachment of sharpshooters to repel possible boarders, and a reporter from the St. Louis *Democrat*—and issued his instructions. The guns were to be secured and the gun ports and other apertures firmly closed against the escape of light. Absolute silence was to be maintained. Acting Master Hoel was to take station out on the hurricane deck, where he could best observe the river and direct navigation. Pilots Daniel Weaver and John Deming were assigned to the wheel.

At 8 P.M. the *Carondelet* moved upstream about a mile to where the loaded barge was held in readiness. Promptly at 10 P.M. the lines were cast off and the ironclad, with her clumsy appendage lashed to her port side, moved out into the current.

Heavy clouds had been gathering to the southward all evening and a line squall, backed by violent lightning and heavy rain, was advancing rapidly upriver. As the *Carondelet* drew abreast of the silenced redoubt the storm broke over her with great violence.

KNOX COLLEGE, COURTESY *Life*

The Currier & Ives view above looks south along the river from just above the sand bar in the map below. This was the scene between March 17 and April 4, 1862, with Foote's gunboats and his mortar scows—moored along the Missouri mainland at right—pounding away in a futile attempt to reduce Island No. 10, which appears as a thin line of trees across the center background. Behind it, on the Tennessee shore, are rows of Confederate tents. To bypass the Rebels, the Carondelet rounded the point and steered hard to starboard, thus avoiding the guns on the Tennessee bank but braving those on the island's near side.

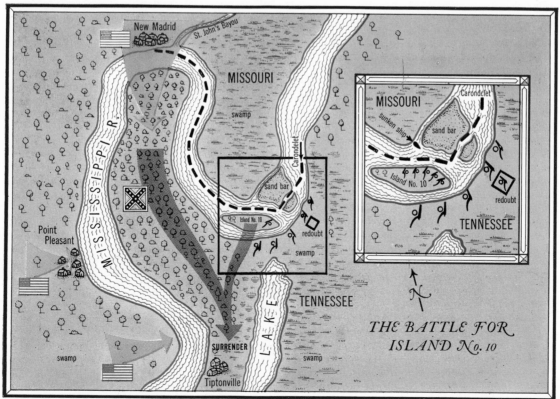

THE BATTLE FOR
ISLAND No. 10

MAP DRAWN FOR AMERICAN HERITAGE BY JOHN TEPPICH

To those watching from upriver she was clearly visible in the almost continuous lightning, and it seemed incredible that she was not discovered by the Confederates. She was holding toward the Missouri side of the river, indicating that Hoel intended to follow the channel across the sand bar, the location of which would be apparent to his experienced eye from the nature of the current. Aboard the gunboat Boatswain's Mate Charles Wilson was now sent forward to take soundings, and Master's Mate Theodore Gilmore was stationed forward on the hurricane deck to pass this information to the pilothouse.

The *Carondelet* had entered the channel and was abreast of Battery No. 2 on the Tennessee shore when flames suddenly shot high into the air from her twin stacks, lighting up the entire scene. Word was hastily passed to Chief Engineer William H. Faulkner to open the flue caps. He did so, and the flames died down. The incident had not been observed on shore, and the expected gunfire did not come. A few minutes later, to everyone's consternation, the stacks flared again. The soot that collected inside them and was normally kept moist by the exhaust steam had become incandescent; loosened by the sudden drafts caused by the passing squall, it had poured flamelike into the open air.

This time the light was seen. Rebel sentries fired their rifles, and signal rockets soared upward from positions on the mainland and the island. A gun was fired in Battery No. 2, followed by a brief silence as the Confederate gunners worked frantically to load and aim their pieces. Within moments firing became general and the low-hanging clouds were illuminated by the flashes of many guns as the Tennessee shore blazed from end to end. The batteries on Island No. 10 now went into action, placing the gunboat under a heavy cross fire.

The *Carondelet* cast all caution aside. "Full steam ahead!" came the order, and as the engineer opened the throttles the rhythmic pounding of the paddles increased to the maximum. Excitement, suspense, and dread gripped the one hundred or more human beings shut within that dark, ill-ventilated floating box. Overhead, thunder cracked and rolled, cannon boomed, shells shrieked by, and bullets "pinged" against the casemate. The torrential rain drummed on the deck above. Each time a furnace door swung open, the glare of the fire danced luridly amid black shadows over gleaming guns and huddled men. The moment the leadsman's report indicated they were clear of the shoal, Hoel put the *Carondelet* hard to starboard and took her down the Missouri channel. It was a demonstration of cool judgment, for as Walke later wrote,

"The *Carondelet* being one of the slowest vessels of the fleet, was difficult to manage, on this occasion particularly she was very hard to steer or turn." A few seconds' delay would have been disastrous. As it was, whether by design or good luck, they just scraped clear, and with the full force of the current behind them, ran down the north side of the island, close under the guns that thundered on the bank above.

The island's guns had not been—perhaps could not be—depressed sufficiently to meet this unexpected maneuver, and as the *Carondelet* rushed by, the shells flew harmlessly over the hurricane deck. Enemy sharpshooters were active, and it was an added miracle that none of the men exposed on the topsides was hit. Four times the ordeal was repeated as the gunboat passed one battery after another. Not one shot hit them: the speed of the gunboat, ten knots or better with the swift current, made it difficult to load and swing the heavy guns in time for a second shot, and the blinding downpour prevented effective aiming.

There was now a brief respite as the *Carondelet* dropped down toward the end of the island. As she passed and drew clear of the battery that faced downstream, her crew momentarily expected the flash of heavy guns astern. Nothing happened—no guns had been mounted in the work! The powerful floating battery still lay ahead, however, and the *Carondelet* now stood over toward the Missouri shore to pass at long range, concealed against the dark profile of the tree-lined shore. A light was visible aboard the battery as they came down, but no guns were fired until they were drawing out of range. Then came eight shots in rapid succession. There were no effective hits, although one ball was later dug out of the hay aboard the barge.

Now that the *Carondelet* was apparently out of danger, silence was relaxed and mutual congratulations were being exchanged, when someone thought to inquire if there was a recognition signal that would identify them to the Union batteries at New Madrid. It would be too bad, after having survived the enemy's guns, to be mistaken for a Rebel gunboat and sent to the bottom by their friends. The batteries at New Madrid were, in fact, expecting to see a signal of red and white lights, but either Walke had not been informed of this, or in the excitement had forgotten it.

Fortunately, Foote had arranged a system of signal guns by which he might learn whether the gunboat had got safely past the island. The *Carondelet* now fired these, and the *Benton* was heard to fire an acknowledgment. This exchange was correctly interpreted at New Madrid, but Walke must have worried, for as they drew inshore before the town, he called loudly through his speaking trumpet, "This is the

CONTINUED ON PAGE 77

72

READING, WRITING, AND HISTORY

By ERIC LARRABEE

The Jungle Trail

The Marauders were a hard-luck outfit from the start. They were conceived in haste, with no past and a dubious future, yet they managed in the face of appalling odds to provide the Second World War with one of its most heroic demonstrations of courage and endurance. These three thousand men were the only American infantry between Italy and New Guinea and the first American ground troops to go into battle on the continent of Asia since the Boxer Rebellion. In a period of three months during 1944 they marched six hundred miles into the jungles of northern Burma, fought five major engagements and seventeen minor ones, and more than amply earned a Distinguished Unit Citation for their "brilliant operation" in capturing the Japanese airfield at Myitkyina.

A terrible price was exacted for their triumph. Less than half of the Marauders finally reached Myitkyina, and these were soon being withdrawn from combat by the medics, as unfit to fight, at a daily rate of seventy-five to a hundred men. To be considered unfit a Marauder then had to be running a fever of over 102 degrees for three consecutive days, and yet at the end

---

The Marauders, by Charlton Ogburn, Jr. Harper & Brothers. 307 pp. $4.50.

---

only two hundred of them could be defined as fit. During their last battle several "fell asleep from sheer exhaustion," writes Charles Ogburn, Jr., and their com-

manding officer "lost consciousness three times while directing it." More had been asked of them than they were able to give.

Whatever it is that makes self-sacrifice of this kind possible, you would not have looked for it in the Marauders' origins and organization. They were an impromptu collection of miscellaneous "volunteers," a word of ironic connotations in the military vocabulary, which meant, in effect, that they could be spared. "The only thing stupider than volunteering is asking for volunteers," said one of their officers. "We've got the misfits of half the divisions in the country." Some were there because they could think of nowhere better to be, and yet some were also there because they simply *liked* combat. Mr. Ogburn, a Marauder himself, tells with awe of the First Battalion commander who suggested, during one of the few lulls between battles, that if nothing else was going to happen they might cross the ridge and fight with the Second Battalion. "He gave a half-laugh, and of course he was joking, but all the same . . . the idea *had* occurred to him."

The Marauders came into being at the Quebec Conference, to which Winston Churchill had cannily decided at the last moment to bring that devout, bearded eccentric, Major General Orde C. Wingate, the apostle of guerrilla warfare by elite troops. Wingate, as Churchill knew he would, made a deep impression on the Americans, and nothing would do but that we too should have a "long-range penetration group," like Wingate's Chindits, and fight alongside them in Burma. In creating these forces the Allied leaders were giving in to the temptation, perilous but understandable, to seek cheap victories. The China-Burma-India theater of war could have only a low priority (initially lower than that of the Caribbean), but perhaps the investment of a small, highly-trained, mobile unit—as Wingate argued—would pay a return there out of all proportion. They decided to chance it, and thus were set in motion the circumstances that brought a number of Americans to places with strange names like Shaduzup and Nhpum Ga and Myitkyina.

The Marauders' worst enemy was their own apprehension, the condition of uninterrupted suspense imposed by a jungle march into enemy country. There is nothing on either side of you, and ahead there is only the next bend in the trail, and after that the next bend, and so on for six hundred miles. Sooner or later, or any moment now, the silence would be broken by the sudden *pup-pup-pup . . . pup-pup-pup-pup* of a Japanese machine gun, and the column would come to a halt. There would be a cry of "Weapons platoon forward . . . clear the trail!" Then perhaps there would be the sound of mortar fire—yours or theirs?— and, shortly, "Medics forward!" until the trail-block was cleared and the column could move on again.

The Marauders lived through this, as Ogburn writes, "not just when it happened but a hundred times a day" in anticipation of it. "Ahead the view was always closed by a bend in the trail. Always there was a bend to be rounded. Each one had to be sweated out. From first to last that was probably the worst part of the campaign for those who had to endure it: *what was around the next bend?*"

Disease was their other enemy, the sores and fevers and dysentery that incapacitated more of the men than Japanese action. "For in the end," as the medical historian of the theater wrote, "amoebas, bacteria, rickettsiae and viruses rather than Japanese soldiers and guns, vanquished the most aggressive, bravest and toughest outfit that fought in the Far East in the Second World War."

Eventually the Marauders came apart, in a fashion considered disgraceful in some higher quarters, and yet Mr. Ogburn's account leaves no question but that they were very poorly treated and that their disintegration was in good part brought about by their superiors. And this is especially paradoxical, inasmuch as they came under the command of "Vinegar Joe," the one American senior officer who should have been expected to sympathize with them the most. Of all American generals, Joseph W. Stilwell was the most demonstrably sympathetic to the ordinary infantry soldier. He tried to comport himself like one, even when this made little sense in a general, and his devotion to the doughboy way-of-war was no façade; it was part and

parcel of his professional experience. But all of this got him nowhere with the Marauders, and it helped *them* not at all.

After the Marauders had made their approach march down the Ledo Road, from India into northern Burma, they pitched camp on an island in the Tarung River, and General Stilwell came wading across to see them. He made a good impression, but there had already been a bad omen. When they had passed his headquarters, having marched 140 miles with full equipment, they had thought he might at least come out and take a few salutes from his only American combat outfit, specially spruced up for the occasion. But he did not do so, thus missing—as Ogburn writes— "the chance for an inexpensive gesture that could have repaid him in days to come."

Later their disappointment turned to unrelieved bitterness. Rightly or wrongly, the heavy moral pressure "just short of outright orders" from his headquarters, to keep in the firing line every American who could pull a trigger, was associated by the Marauders with Stilwell personally. They thought him a small man in a job too large for him, utterly bloodless and lacking in human kindness; and only when the war was long over, and the story of Stilwell's own troubles had begun to be published, did Ogburn himself realize how badly they had misjudged their commander.

The trouble was that he took them for granted. All his life Stilwell had looked forward to leading American troops in combat, but now that the chance had come to him there was too much else for him to do. He was preoccupied, as he saw his mission, with getting the British and the Chinese to fight the Japanese in Burma, and he was filled with a considerable mistrust of their desire to do so. The one thing in his tangled and frustrating existence that he knew he could rely on was American infantry. The Marauders at least he could trust—especially since they were a "picked" unit, led by one of his own best officers—and so he gave them the dirty jobs to do, and pushed them beyond their limit, and wore them out.

The Marauders were then retired to a so-called "rest camp" in India, a totally unprepared pasture surrounded by "bashas" they considered unfit for cattle. They had been told to expect shower baths. One morning some lengths of rusty pipe and a few oil drums were kicked off a truck, and those were their showers, while a few miles away soldiers who had never heard the whine of a hostile's bullet enjoyed comfortable quarters and concrete shower stalls, and in New Delhi officers had electric fans and refrigerators. The Marauders blew up. With the assistance of a local distilled product called Bull-Fight Brandy—proscribed, unsuccessfully, by the medics—they began to tear apart hospitals, Red

Cross canteens, and their own quarters. Orders were impossible to enforce, threats meant nothing, and they went AWOL in quantity. The strain of the disreputable, which had been their strength, now did them in.

There is the question of how valuable a special-purpose organization like the Marauders can ever be. The British Field Marshal Sir William Slim, who was in practice Stilwell's superior officer and understood him better than did many Americans, thought that neither the Marauders nor Orde Wingate's Chindits ever quite justified their moral and physical cost: "Both forces . . . had been subjected to intense strain, both had unwisely been promised that their ordeal would be short, and both were asked to do more than was possible." Slim believes that these *corps d'élite*, while they may give a magnificent account of themselves, are wrong in principle. "The level of initiative, individual training, and weapon skill required in, say, a commando, is admirable; what is not admirable is that it should be confined to a few small units. . . . Armies do not win wars by means of a few bodies of super-soldiers but by the average quality of their standard units. Anything, whatever short cuts to victory it may promise, which thus weakens the Army spirit, is dangerous."

The fate of the Marauders can be interpreted as support for this hard doctrine, yet that would not be the whole story. True, they were formed in defiance of the rules. They did not even have the consolation of a glamorous name, like the Queen's Own Royal West Kent Regiment, or of the military tinsel—promotions and decorations—that can mean so much to men in danger. "Merrill's Marauders" was the subsequent invention of a journalist, and they knew only that they belonged to something with the absurd and clumsy title of 5307th Composite Unit (Provisional)—hardly an inspiring device to bear on one's banner (it led one Marauder to inquire, in a moment of stress, what had happened to the other five-thousand-three-hundred-and-six composite units). They had no sense of continuity, and they were terrifyingly alone—as though the Army, not to mention the nation, had forgotten them. Virtually their only assets, from the orthodox point of view, were their officers and a well-conceived tactical plan. For the rest, they had only themselves, and the true moral of their private victory over the orthodox is that in the balance this was enough.

On the Far Shore

While the issue at Myitkyina was still in doubt, there began on the other side of the world a contest of a wholly different character—the Normandy invasion, the seaborne assault across the English Channel now known by the generic name of D Day. This was the largest and most carefully planned military operation in history. There had never been, and there will never be again, anything quite like it. For the number of men, aircraft, and ships involved; for the bulk and complexity of their equipment; for the calculation and intelligent control required to employ them—for these and more the invasion has no equal. D Day was the supreme expression of the classic military art.

The requirements of a modern soldier in the field, with the proper weapons and clothing, in themselves demand a large industrial capacity; and on D Day they were multiplied by the many thousands. The statistics are so far out of the ordinary as to seem unreal. On the American beaches alone, on the first day, we were planning to land the equivalent of two hundred train-

---

D Day, the Sixth of June, 1944, by David Howarth. McGraw-Hill. 251 pp. $4.95.

---

loads of troops. These would be followed, in the next two weeks, by enough vehicles to form a double line from Pittsburgh to Chicago, and by twice as many American soldiers as there had been in the entire United States Army in 1939. Fitting together the pieces of this enormous jigsaw puzzle was so complicated that an early operational order of the First Army alone had more words in it than *Gone with the Wind*.

All of southern England had become an armed camp. So many were the miles of military stores, of tanks and trucks lined up, that the island seemed weighted down with them and, as someone suggested at the time, but for the barrage balloons, would have sunk. The writers who have described the build-up for D Day frequently fall back on one particular phrase for it—they speak of the coiling of a great spring. D Day was a mechanism being wound up, a repository of condensed and organized energy waiting to be released. Surely it is this that gives such drama to General Eisenhower's final decision whether or not to go: the fact that so much accumulated power could wait on a single word.

Hardest of all to recapture now is the feeling that D Day might have failed. Yet it might have. We see the industrial potential of Great Britain and North America matched against that of German Europe, which was exhausting itself in the struggle with Russia, and we wonder how we could have doubted the outcome. We know now that the Germans' "Atlantic Wall" was weak, and forget that the Normandy beaches were nonetheless more heavily defended than Iwo Jima, Tarawa, or Peleliu. Something could always go wrong. Plans have to be made in the expectation of sloth, inaccuracy, the eternal cussedness of things, or that inherent military tendency toward chaos expressed by the word "snafu." And the commander, most of all, must be so prepared for this that the possibility of it is constantly within his perspective. Fortunately, General Eisenhower allowed to be preserved the dispatch he privately wrote out for himself beforehand, and kept in his wallet, for it is a most valuable and characteristic document:

Our landings in the Cherbourg-Havre area have failed to gain a satisfactory foothold and I have withdrawn the troops. My decision to attack at this time and place was based upon the best information available. The troops, the air, and the Navy did all that bravery and devotion to duty could do. If any blame or fault attaches to the attempt it is mine alone.

For a commander of Eisenhower's caliber must never forget that everything finally hinges on the single soldier. The D-Day juggernaut was overpowering in the abstract; but in reality, on Omaha Beach on D-Day morning, it was a cluster of demoralized and disorganized men, huddled in the shelter of a shallow ridge of gravel from the vicious fire of well-protected defenders. The fine, forward cutting edge of the great machine was wet and scared and sick and wounded and dying; and now all the orderly, impressive planning had come to nothing but risk and ignorance and makeshift. Something did go wrong. There were more German troops than expected, the neutralizing barrage didn't neutralize, the floatable tanks didn't float, the boats came in on the wrong beaches, the engineers didn't get time to clear away the obstacles—and before long there was disaster in the making.

This is the D Day to which David Howarth has devoted his book, not the D Day of strategy and logistics but of individuals and what happened to them. He has chosen to pick several dozen—American, British, German, French—and follow them through a range of experiences that in sum describes that day, at least to the extent that anything so vast and varied can be described at all. For example, we see it momentarily through the eyes of a German soldier named Erwin Müller, who had been posted on guard that night, and was peering over a garden gate, when suddenly the whole sky to the south and west was filled with parachutes and he knew that the war was lost. Later he and three other Germans captured two of the chutists, and a third who was badly hurt. "How far is it to Paris, fella?" asked one of them, and gave him a bar of chocolate. Then the Americans closed the eyes of their companion and crossed his arms on his chest, and the six men from the two armies, in their respective languages, said the Lord's Prayer for him.

Howarth has a nice sense of military realism, which enables him to see how even mistakes and confusion can have their uses. The American air-drop was badly scattered, which should have been wrong, but its effect was right: during about eight hours that night and morning the Germans at one end of the beachhead were virtually paralyzed. Their telephones were going dead, their dispatch riders were riding off into the dark and disappearing. Howarth describes this as a "gigantic and lethal game of hide and seek," in which "the Americans knew what was happening, but few of them knew where they were; the Germans knew where they were, but none of them knew what was happening. . . . Of course, the German divisions were more heavily armed than the Americans, but their artillery and even their tanks, in these early hours, were useless. Ten thousand Americans, spread over a hundred square miles of country and constantly moving, never offered a target worth a shell."

Howarth also has a warm and deep sympathy for the human aspect of D Day, and for what it meant to people back home in England. He is not ashamed of sentiment, which is a fortunate thing in a writer who must tell you how the invasion was announced during the day in the English factories, and how the women—few of whom were without a husband or son or brother they had not recently heard from—wept over their work. There is an inalterable drama about the expenditure of wealth and daring on so large a scale that even the most tame and depleted account cannot diminish, and Mr. Howarth's is not tame. Best of all, he gives the sense of what it felt like, anywhere in southern England on the night before that decisive dawn, to wake up and hear passing overhead the greatest fleet of aircraft that anyone had ever heard, or is likely to hear again.

There will be no more D Days; the atomic bomb will see to that. An invasion fleet is one of the few targets that "justifies," in the amoral military sense, a nuclear weapon; and against an enemy so armed, any such concentrated effort will in the future be suicidal. But the quality of it will endure. From the Marauders to the D-Day invasion fleet is only a step of magnitude, just as it is only a step of magnitude from the invasion fleet to the terrible forces poised today. What is memorable about the men on Omaha Beach is that eventually they moved forward. A lieutenant stood up and said, to nobody in particular, "Are you going to lay there and get killed, or get up and do something about it?" and before long scattered groups had begun to work their way inland. "Nobody will ever know how many groups started and failed," writes Mr. Howarth. "Roughly a dozen succeeded." In the balance, they were enough.

U.S. gunboat *Carondelet*." At that moment, a mistake in signals between pilothouse and engine room put the boat hard aground fifty yards from the landing. All hands immediately went to work to shift the heavy guns aft. It took an hour to lighten the bow sufficiently, and it was 1 A.M. before they backed off and went alongside the bank at a spot that a lighted fire indicated as the landing place. They had taken three hours to make the trip down. During thirty minutes of that time they had passed through the fire of some sixty guns and had emerged unscathed. Grog was issued to all hands.

Events now began to move rapidly. General Pope requested that Walke destroy the battery of 64-pounders located at Watson's landing. He also notified Walke that another gunboat would soon be sent down, if conditions were favorable. An early morning thunderstorm provided the opportunity, and the *Pittsburgh* ran down past Island No. 10, starting at 2 A.M. April 7 and arriving at New Madrid three hours later. One would expect the Confederates to have been on the alert this time, and to have given the *Pittsburgh* a very rough time indeed. They did their best, firing as rapidly as possible with every gun that could be brought into action, but failed to register a single hit.

The presence of the two Union ironclads on the lower stretch of the river altered the complexion of affairs for the Confederates, who now deployed their troops in the woods back of the landing places. They were not seriously worried, however, as Pope did not appear capable of mounting an attack of real importance with only two gunboats to ferry his troops across.

But the Rebels had underestimated Pope's cunning. Some days before, one of his divisional commanders had suggested that a canal be cut across the peninsula formed by the bend opposite Island No. 10 so that light-draft transports and supply barges could be brought down to New Madrid out of range of Confederate guns. Pope had approved the scheme, the canal had been cut, and its existence kept secret.

Now, suddenly, the surprised Confederates saw four transports, crawling with "bluebellies" and bristling with bayonets, steam out from their hiding place in St. John's Bayou and head for Watson's Landing. The Rebels were now boxed in on both flanks, with the river in front and the swamps to the rear. Word was hastily passed up and down the shore—"Every man for himself." A few hundred managed to make their way through the swamps, or to float down river on planks and hastily made rafts, but the bulk of the Confeder-

ate troops surrendered on the spot without resistance.

The bag included General Mackall and two other general officers; troops estimated at nearly seven thousand; seven thousand stand of small arms; about one hundred guns, half of them of heavy caliber; and a vast quantity of ammunition and other supplies. The Union also acquired a fleet of handsome river steamers. Pope's casualties totaled fifty-four.

The sudden collapse of a position that the Confederacy had confidently expected to hold out indefinitely brought consternation to the South and indignation at the manner in which the affair had been conducted. It was universally considered that at the

A key to Union victory was the two-mile channel cut between the upper river and the bayous leading to New Madrid. On forty-foot rafts teams of four men worked a pivoting underwater saw, cutting off trees below the surface to enable light-draft troop transports to bypass the guns of Island No. 10.

least the store of ammunition and supplies should have been prevented from falling into the hands of the enemy. An effort was made to save the floating battery—it was cut loose with its crew on board and drifted down river exchanging shots with Union batteries—but it ran aground at Point Pleasant, a total wreck and an object of curiosity to the Union troops.

The *Carondelet* served honorably on the western rivers throughout the war, her last great action being to reinforce General George H. Thomas' assault at Nashville in December of 1864. She and the other Union ironclads helped prove the feasibility of combined land and naval operations against entrenched land forts—a strategic concept which eventually won the Mississippi and split the Confederacy in two.

Phillips Melville, a retired Air Force colonel, is now a free-lance writer and illustrator. He contributed "Eleven Guns for the Grand Union" to the October, 1958, issue of AMERICAN HERITAGE.

New York Ferry Boats

CONTINUED FROM PAGE 31

panorama of thousands of twinkling lights and ghostly forms of ships and silent multitudes of closely packed buildings—a Manhattan unbelievably asleep—as the *Maryland* rounded the Battery and pointed her nose across the Hudson!

Today New York's ferryboats are vanishing; where yesterday there were ten, there is now only one. Many of their slips, with salt-encrusted, yielding wooden walls, have vanished completely. Others, unpainted and untended, are rotting away. Only the Manhattan-Staten Island line still functions on the old heroic scale, and bridges already join Staten Island to New Jersey. Soon there will be another bridge from Staten Island to Long Island to cut the traffic further and perhaps end the existing ferry from Staten Island to Brooklyn.

No boat at all crosses the East River today. Gone are the once-busy South Street Ferry and Hamilton Ferry, which used to cross the eastern part of New York Harbor, where it is joined by the East River, to transport passengers to various parts of Brooklyn. Gone is the Wall Street Ferry. And gone, likewise, is that teeming focus of metropolitan traffic of other days, the Fulton Ferry. Long after the shadow of the East River Bridge first fell across its boats, they continued to ply undaunted—but, as the years passed, that shadow became ever more symbolic of what was certain to happen to them on some forthcoming and less enlightened day.

The crowning irony for the two (until spring, 1959, it was three) remaining Hudson River ferry lines is that they offer, quite unsuspected by millions of New York drivers, a sometimes faster and cheaper rush-hour service than the highways. While traffic inches through the teeming tunnels, often taking a half-hour or more, fast ferry service operates at frequent intervals, half-empty, in the breezes up above. The very existence of these ferries, except to regular railway commuters, is barely known. There are no highway signs leading to them; the terminals are hidden in dingy corners, their existence kept dark; there is no word on the radio that tries to guide harried drivers; even the police are vague about them. All of this probably suits the railway owners, the Lackawanna and the Jersey Central, who would like to be out of a business made unprofitable by government. Cities are planned for the motorcar nowadays, not for ferries, nor for the fresh-air lover, nor even for the pedestrian.

Now that the shape of things to come has, to such a horrifying extent, arrived, the ferry has no more future in the city than comfort itself. It is only an amenity, something unknown to modern-day city planners, a whiff of the sea, a breath of cool air and a suggestion of romance at the beginning and end of the day. After the last ferry is scrapped, however, some city department may think to build a replica, of modern design of course, in Central Park for the children. It will have an imitation whistle, and Muzak.

Pilgrims and Puritans CONTINUED FROM PAGE 52

more than half of which he took over with him. Mostly theology, since he had to preach thrice a week; the rest practical—herbals, books of surveying and medicine, works on the culture of silkworms and varieties of timber. But, in addition, were these worldly authors: Machiavelli's *Prince,* Bodin's *Republic,* Bacon's *Advancement of Learning,* and Raleigh's *Prerogatives of Parliaments in England.*

For company there was Miles Standish and a much younger man, Edward Winslow; and Governor Bradford, to whom Elder Brewster stood second in the little colony. Miles Standish was born about 1584, of a younger branch of an old Lancashire family, probably the Duxbury branch, after which he called his place in New England. Before 1603 he was already a lieutenant under Vere in the Netherlands. A professional soldier, he joined the Pilgrims as such, for in religion he was never one of them. He was given command of parties exploring the country and defending the colony against suspect Indians—on one occasion being responsible for a deed of blood against some Indian chiefs. In 1621 he was made captain of the colony, and was frequently an assistant to the governor. Next to Standish in dealing with the Indians was Winslow, also a man of good family, who when traveling on the Continent joined the Leyden community.

Above all there was Governor Bradford: impossible to overestimate what the Plymouth plantation owed to him, for he was, like Winthrop, ideally suited to govern. They would not have been the great men they became if they had remained at home in England: no scope, no opportunity. Bradford brought with him the same Elizabethan ideas of authority that Winthrop enjoyed: the generality share in government "only in some weighty matters, when we think good." Queen Elizabeth I might have subscribed to that.

As a youth affected by the preaching of Richard Clifton, William Bradford joined the Scrooby flock and went with Robinson to Leyden. He was of a spirit to dislike sectarian labels and wished to retain fellowship with all reformed churches. This was too much for some, but Bradford thought it "great arrogancy for any man or church to think that he or they have so sounded the word of God to the bottom." He was re-elected governor thirty times, almost continuously in fact—in spite of the fear of the New England colonies of a governor for life—and it is obvious that the Pilgrims could not get on without him: his long rule was really one of a benevolent autocracy.

Though not a university man, he was well read, and indeed as a historian to good purpose; for his *History of Plymouth Plantation* is held to be a masterpiece. In his well-stocked library he, too, had Bodin, Guicciardini's *History of Florence*, and Peter Martyr's *Decades of the New World*. It is nice to think that this Puritan governor, so wise, so sober, so restrained, an "achieved spirit," as his age would say, also owned a red waistcoat with silver buttons, a colored hat, and a violet cloak. But it is by his *History* that he lives, for it offers us the perfect mirror of the life of the Pilgrim colony.

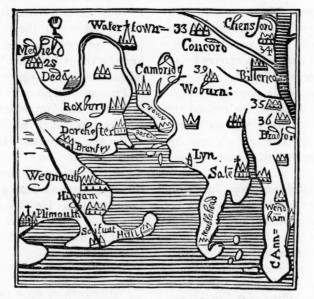

Massachusetts Bay in 1667. North is to the right.

It has indeed the qualities that give enduring life to a book: absolute fidelity, lifelikeness and trustworthiness; its moral purity—the selflessness, submission, and control—shines through. Its tones are, however, those of a New England winter, russet and gray and white, where one may prefer color and poetry. Perhaps there is a sober, subdued poetry in Bradford, and the book certainly has charm: like all living work it carries the personality of its author.

For the Elizabethan background of Massachusetts we could not do better than look at the life lived at Groton in the years before John Winthrop left for America. All the Winthrops were given to writing—letters, diaries, journals—so it is well documented. We derive an agreeable impression of their family life in the pleasant undulating pastures in that nook of East Anglia.

The Winthrops were originally clothiers. Adam Winthrop, the Governor's grandfather, describes himself in his will as clothworker of London, gentleman of Groton—where he lies again under his brass, taken away to America in the last century, restored in this. His son Adam, bred to the law, became auditor of Trinity and St. John's Colleges, Cambridge. His diary shows him paying his obligations on Groton church porch, for the poor or to the collectors of a subsidy or for setting forth a soldier to the wars. We note his payments indoors and outdoors, for a new plow or half a dozen skins of parchment, settles for the hall, pairs of shoes and books for young John.

In the son we observe a more intense and introspective religious consciousness, and this state of mind was not improved by the deaths of two wives in as many years, for John Winthrop was distinctly uxorious.

It was at this time, in this year 1616, that he began to keep a record of his spiritual state, from which we gain an authentic picture of a Puritan's inner mind. John Winthrop felt that his heart halted between God and the world, that he was not yet "resolved upon the denial of this world and myself." His *Experiencia* shows us how hard he tried. After the affliction of his second wife's death he thought he "had brought under my rebellious flesh and prettily tamed it by moderate and spare diet and holding it somewhat close to its task, by prayer, reading, meditation and the works of my calling." He was a busy justice of the peace, but at sessions he refrained his "mouth, eyes, and ears from vanity as well as I could while I was there."

Nevertheless, when he tried to settle down to his ordinary tasks again, he found that "the flesh had gotten head and heart again and began to linger after the world; the society of the saints seemed a contemptible thing, meditations were few, prayer was tedious, and fain would the flesh have been at an end before I began." He put himself on a spare diet again and set himself to read devout books. After some time at this, he was surprised to find that he "grew very melancholic and uncomfortable," especially since he had refrained from any "outward conversation in the world." In this condition he began to enjoy experiences like those of a Counter-Reformation mystic, such as St. John of the Cross or St. Theresa. He had such "a heavenly meditation of the love between Christ and me as ravished my heart with unspeakable joy; methought my soul had as familiar and sensible society with him as my wife could have with the kindest husband. I desired no other happiness but to be embraced of him." And, very shortly, he was: "O my Lord, my love, how wholly delectable art thou! Let him kiss me with the kisses of his mouth, for his love is sweeter than wine; how lovely is thy countenance! how pleasant are thy embracings!"

This state of exaltation seems to have ended with his third marriage—and perhaps it was about time—in 1618, when this spiritual diary comes to an end. Winthrop got away from this disagreeable intensity of morbid introspection; his impulses found normal channels of expression; he was able to turn himself to the extrovert tasks of a legal career. He became an attorney in the Court of Wards and a member of the Inner Temple. It would seem that it was external considerations that decided him to go to America—the state of the country, the loss of his post; the King's decision to dispense with Parliament, his embarking upon personal rule, meant that there was no future for Puritans while that lasted. The outlook was indeed gloomy; Winthrop's response to it may be read in a letter to his third wife. "I am verily persuaded God will bring some heavy affliction upon this land, and that speedily . . . if the Lord seeth it will be good for us, he will provide a shelter and a hiding-place for us and others, as a Zoar for Lott."

Of those who met together at Cambridge in August, 1629, and entered into an agreement to go, Thomas Dudley was twelve years and Sir Richard Saltonstall two years Winthrop's senior; William Pynchon and Increase Nowell his junior by two years and William Vassall by four years. All of these men were Elizabethans, formed in that age.

Dudley, born at Northampton in 1576, was the son of a captain "slain in the wars." Left an orphan but with a sufficient maintenance, he went to a grammar school and became a page in the household of the Earl of Northampton. In turn he went to the wars to serve as captain under Henry IV, but saw no fighting, for peace was made; that, then, would be 1598. In 1603 he married, according to Cotton Mather, "a gentlewoman both of good estate and good extraction."

Becoming steward to the Puritan Earl of Lincoln, in nine years Dudley succeeded in paying off the estate's debt of £20,000 and arranged a marriage of the young Earl with a daughter of the still more Puritan Lord Saye and Sele. Now

Seal of the Plymouth Colony.

well off, Dudley retired to Boston in Lincolnshire to enjoy the ministrations of the Reverend John Cotton. In close touch with all the discussions preparatory to the move, he sailed on the *Arbella*—a more important ship than the *Mayflower,* for she carried Winthrop and the Massachusetts leadership on board. Though Winthrop's deputy-governor, Dudley had a violent quarrel with him over the decision to move from their first site to Boston. They exchanged some very ungodly, though not necessarily unpuritanical, words; the fact was that the two men were hardly congenial to each other.

Dudley was dogmatic and overbearing; he had none of Winthrop's moderation, judgment, charm—for there is a certain charm in the personality of Winthrop. Once and again they came in conflict—there were people who disapproved of Winthrop's wise leniency; but the terms of mutual submission with which they terminated their dispute are a tribute to the efficacy of Puritan discipline in self-restraint and self-control. A man of fifty-four when he landed in New England, Dudley was tough physically: he produced progeny at the age of seventy. He was four times elected governor, thirteen times deputy-governor; he was one of the first overseers of Harvard, one of the two Massachusetts commissioners who formed the New England Confederation. He was something of a scholar and, like most Elizabethans, wrote verse. A last poem, found in his pocket after his death, spoke his mind on toleration:

Let men of God in courts and churches watch
O'er such as do a toleration *hatch.*

These lines were not without application to such as Saltonstall. Nephew to Sir Richard Saltonstall, who had been Lord Mayor of London, owner of the manor of Ledsham and a justice of the peace, he was one of the Puritan governing class who went over on the *Arbella.* But he did not see eye to eye with the rigid exclusiveness of the theocracy, and was twice fined for backslidings in regard to church matters. Perhaps this helped to persuade him to return home next year: *he* had not burnt his boats. He never went back to Massachusetts, though he obtained a grant of land in Connecticut; his progeny continued the line in New England. From wicked Old England he remonstrated later with the Reverend John Cotton and the Reverend John Wilson for their harsh attitude to the Quakers.

Of those only just junior to Winthrop—Pynchon, Nowell, Vassall—all three had trouble with the ruling authorities. Pynchon became a member of the first court of assistants and helped to found Roxbury. In 1636 he withdrew from Massachusetts along with the Reverend Thomas Hooker, who found the infallibility of the Reverend John Cotton too much for him. They were then charged by Cotton with breaking their covenant by departing. Later Pynchon, who had founded Springfield, withdrew it from the rule of Connecticut. Thereupon Hooker accused him of breaking the covenant, in the same terms Cotton had used. He had no better luck with Massachusetts. When Pynchon wrote a book in 1650 controverting the Calvinist view of the Atonement, the General Court ordered the book to be burnt and the author to appear before them. This he refused to do; "instead, he decided to return to England, where he might enjoy that liberty of opinion which was denied him in the colony he had helped to found."

In 1633 there came over the two authoritative religious leaders of the first generation, Cotton and Thomas Hooker. The same boat contained them, though the same pulpit on arrival did not. They had been invited over together, but it was wisely decided that "a couple of such great men might be more serviceable asunder than together." Samuel Stone accompanied them, so that it was possible to say, in the punning manner of the time, that in Massachusetts they now had "Cotton for their clothing, Hooker for their fishing, and Stone for their building."

The important Cotton was probably the leading nonconforming clergyman in, if it is not paradoxical to say so, the Church of England. We have seen that he became vicar of the English Boston, where he soon began to simplify the services in the interest of more preaching—he was a great preacher. He soon developed a faithful following, dependent on his ministrations; he, like Winthrop, was a leader—and this was given full scope in Massachusetts, where, Roger Williams said, there were people who "could hardly believe that God would suffer Mr. Cotton to err." Everybody else erred at some time; Mr. Cotton never.

He and Winthrop were both Elizabethans in their point of view; they were both men whose minds were geared to government. Cotton's chief works were in defense of the civil power's right to interfere in support of the truth. (This was just what the government in England believed in.) What Cotton pronounced was apt to become the law of the land—except when, given the job of drawing up a code of laws, he came out with the complete Mosaic system, of a draconian severity. This had to be rejected by the laity, who showed more sense. But Cotton had no more illusions than Winthrop as to the people's fitness to govern:

"Democracy," he wrote, "I do not conceive that ever God did ordain as a fit government either for church or commonwealth." Nevertheless, there was in Protestantism an inner dynamic that led on to democracy—in particular in Congregationalism, with the emphasis on the consent of the congregation, if highly select; and this shortly became evident in New England.

Thomas Hooker, the son of a Leicestershire yeoman, was a student at Queen's College, Cambridge, and became, like Cotton, a fellow of Emmanuel. At Esher in Surrey, to which living he was presented by Francis Drake, his patron's wife lay under the impression that she had committed the unpardonable sin—whatever that was (something sexual and absurd, no doubt, one can imagine). Hooker succeeded in comforting her, where others had failed, Hooker had a way with him—to the soul—and married the lady's waiting woman: the proper social status for a clergyman's bride.

Hooker and Stone were called as pastor and teacher of Newtown. But they and their congregation became restive under the self-sufficient autocracy of Massachusetts. It used to be thought that they were democrats. As to that, Samuel Stone, whose later life was embittered by a long controversy with the ruling elder of his church, spoke succinctly: he held the essence of Congregationalism to be "a *speaking* aristocracy in the face of a *silent* democracy."

Hooker's sermon at the making of the Connecticut constitution used to be thought a democratic declaration, when he stated that the "foundation of all authority is the free consent of the people." But we recognize in that the traditional social-contract doctrine as the base of society. "They who have the power to appoint officers and magistrates," he wrote, "it is in their power also to set the bounds and limitations of the power and place unto which they call them." We recognize in that a continuing element in American society, the heart of American political conviction.

The bent of Hooker's mind was, however, evangelical, toward what is called saving souls: his books bear such titles as *The Soul's Preparation for Christ, The Soul's Vocation, The Soul's Implantation,* etc. From Connecticut Hooker was called to take part in the controversies that raged in Massachusetts over the tiresome Roger Williams and the exceptionally self-satisfied Mrs. Hutchinson, the Antinomian. That far-from-quiet Quietist, spilling her spiritual favors all round her, played a part in New England comparable with that of Madame Guyon at the court of Louis XIV. The New England theocracy had no more hesitation in shutting up the one than the French bishops had the other: the New England version of an episcopate was no less responsible for keeping order in the nursery.

Roger Williams did not agree, but then he never agreed with anybody, including himself, for long. As for order in the nursery, in a sense he never emerged from it. Since he was a man entirely of the seventeenth century, there is no need to go further into his career—only insofar as his conflict with the Elizabethan views of Cotton brings out the character of the latter. No sooner had Williams landed in Massachusetts than he discovered that he was "once more in a land where the non-conforming were unfree." He responded by declaring that civil governments had no right to enforce religious injunctions, and when the civil authorities showed that they had the power, he took refuge in Plymouth. He inconveniently attacked the "imperialism" of the Puritan colonists, for of course their pushing out the Indians was "imperialism" of an uncompromising sort. This troubled the sensitive conscience of Roger Williams, who adored Red Indians. Banished from Massachusetts, he escaped in midwinter to their friendly shelter and founded a settlement in Providence, the beginning of Rhode Island. Imperial Massachusetts sought to extinguish Rhode Island and invade it; only an appeal to Old England secured a patent and freedom for it to exist.

It was while enjoying the freedom of the old country that Roger Williams engaged in his famous controversy with Cotton. Cotton had issued his encyclical *Letter concerning the Power of the Magistrate in Matters of Religion.* To this Williams replied with *The Bloody Tenet of Persecution for Cause of Conscience.* The affronted Cotton rejoined with *The Bloody Tenet Washed and made White in the Blood of the Lamb.* Williams, inexplicably unabashed, wound up with *The Bloody Tenet yet more Bloody by Cotton's Endeavour to wash it white in the Blood of the Lamb.* This was the kind of thing that New England delighted in bothering its head about. Yet these were real issues, and Roger Williams' ideas lived on to win the battle at a later date.

The Puritans went out to set a model of a godly commonwealth for the world to see and follow. They suffered the fate of all who make an egoistic, a conceited assumption as to the course history will take: the course it takes is never what they suppose it will be. They are always disappointed—but they ask for disillusionment, to assume so boldly, so confidently, that things are going to go the way they think. The godly in England, like Milton, suffered the bitter surprise that the country did not want them but the King

The famous "pine tree" shilling, among the earliest coins to be minted by New England colonists.

again, the ungodly Restoration. Similarly with New England—the second generation there wondered what had gone wrong.

Nevertheless all experience does not go for nothing; not everything—the heroic effort, the sacrifice—had been in vain. The continuing legacy of the Elizabethan Puritans to New England, though different from what they expected, was a matter of the highest importance in the constitution of the greatest of modern nations. It did not turn out the New Jerusalem, but it turned out to provide the strongest of bonds to bind together a continental society of a new sort and kind. Something very strong, even astringent, was needed to hold together so vast a country—the New England mentality, something very wiry and taut and idiosyncratic; something which, when it lost the narrowness of its early beliefs, retained a distinguishing element—strongly ethical, seeing life in terms of obligation and duty rather than pleasure, social responsibility and doing good, neighborliness and goodness. Though the theology and belief had gone, the metaphysics broken down, the Puritan character remained—the strongest factor in survival; for, in history, to survive is what matters.

The overwhelmingly, the excruciatingly theological complexion of the intellectual culture of New England did but reflect not so much Elizabethan England as Elizabethan Puritanism. Massachusetts was the realization of the dreams of its later, rather than earlier, generation. We must not underrate their intellectual energy, even if we do not relish the forms it took. The Puritans were intolerant in their day, and in consequence they have met with an intolerance in ours, reluctant to do them justice for what they achieved. Samuel Eliot Morison tells us that "the dominant Puritan clergy, far from being indifferent to culture . . . did everything possible under the circumstances under which they lived, to stimulate, promote and even produce intellectual activity. Moreover, it was largely the clergy who persuaded a poor and struggling people to set up schools and a college which continued to serve the community in later centuries."

Their handicaps in keeping civilized standards going were tremendous—theirs was a pioneer country strenuously engaged in the struggle for existence, a whole Atlantic away from the centers of learning. It is all the more astonishing what they achieved, whether one likes it or not. Within ten years of its founding, Massachusetts had a vigorous intellectual life of its own. No other English commonwealth attempted to provide for learning so soon after it was founded—not even the States of the Union two centuries later, as the frontier advanced. But New England had Elizabethan England behind it, with its enthusiasm for education, fortified by the Puritan belief in intellect. New Englanders proved their belief not only in their precepts but in their works: they were ready to tax themselves for things which in Old England were provided by endowment.

These were the things of the mind, and their minds were formed by the English universities, especially by Cambridge, from which nearly all the leaders came. The Puritan migration contained a very high proportion of university men; up to 1646 there were a hundred Cambridge men to some thirty from Oxford. There was an average of one university man to every forty or fifty families—much higher, we may say, than in Old England.

Puritanism throve "under conditions of vigor, hardship and isolation"; the tensions within the New England mind resulted in a higher average of intellectual activity. Morison tells us that Puritanism "preserved far more of the humanist tradition than did non-Puritanism in the other English colonies." It devoted more attention to classical scholarship and had an interest therefore in making verses, such as all English students were taught to write. So too with literary form and style: Morison points out that "the older founders of New England grew up in the age of Shakespeare and the King James Bible," and in consequence these men "wrote prose superior by any standard to that of the later, native-born writers."

However, we must not allow ourselves to be overpersuaded by the charm of a great historian. Shakespeare was precisely what the New England Puritans excluded. They would have suppressed the Elizabethan drama if they could. They had no appreciation of the majesty of the Catholic Church, the Rome of Sixtus V, the music of Palestrina. They had nothing but dislike for the grave and ordered beauty of the Anglican Church, the cadences of the Book of Common Prayer, the music of Byrd and Orlando Gibbons, their contemporaries; there is no evidence that they had any liking for the music of that golden age, the wonders of their time, Tallis and Dowland and Wilbye. (The Catholics had; they contributed largely to it.)

The Puritan attitude involved a profound contraction of response to life, in some ways a denial of life. They were enemies to the glorification of the natural man, with all his instincts and appetites, that characterized the Renaissance and the great Elizabethans, the discovery of a new world of riches in himself to match that in the outer world across the oceans.

The early literature of the Puritans shows best in the writings of their historians—the sincerity and truthfulness, prime qualities for a historian, of Bradford and Winthrop. But what a story they had on hand to write! Then, shortly, after the winter, they would be putting forth shoots of poetry, naïve, musical, delightful—with Anne Bradstreet—as a bird's song.

On the other hand, some contraction of response, some repression, some inhibition, produces greater strength and energy with which to face the ills of life, particularly in the harsh, sad conditions of pioneer life in the wilderness. One sees, with more imaginative sympathy, what it all meant for them as one stands in the museum devoted to them at Plymouth, surrounded by the rude objects of their daily use, or by the graveyards, touching in their simplicity, by the roadside in country places, or in the village streets of New England. And for the life of their community, in probity and public spirit, in moral responsibility and uprightness, in humaneness as to punishment and in mutual help in need, in simple godliness—whether we believe or no, regarding it as a human fact—they did exemplify higher standards than any other English society. And theirs more than any others' was the making of the nation.

This is the fourth of five articles specially prepared for AMERICAN HERITAGE *by A. L. Rowse, a leading British authority on the Elizabethan Age. The fifth and last—on America in Elizabethan art, science, and literature—will appear in December. The series will form a part of his book,* The Elizabethans and America, *which Harper & Brothers will publish this month.*

PROBLEMS, PROBLEMS, PROBLEMS

On Tuesday Night the Fifth Instant, some evil-minded Persons stole out of the Garden of Nathanael Wardell, Chaise-maker, a Necessary-House, and carried it away. Whoever will discover the Person or Persons that did it, so as they may be brought to Justice and convicted thereof, shall have Ten Pounds Reward.

Boston *News-Letter*, October 7, 1736, reprinted by courtesy of the *William and Mary Quarterly*, January, 1959.

The War to End War

CONTINUED FROM PAGE 6

broken and plastered across his chest as in prayer. Both legs had been fractured, and they too were in plaster. He could speak through clenched teeth, and he could wiggle the toes on his right foot. Thus accoutered, he entered the life of the hospital ward, which was teeming, after hours, with vigorous dice games and Martinique rum. He soon won a considerable sum in the dice games.

The lieutenant made his own casts of the dice, a brother officer placing the dice beneath the swollen toes for the lieutenant to wiggle, meanwhile holding a mirror so that he might "read 'em and weep." He soon found that the raw *rhum Negrito,* sucked through his glass tube, was too fiery on his jaw wounds; and so a rubber drainage tube was acquired, being inserted in his nostril toward the esophagus, well past the fractured area. Then with a fellow lieutenant holding a small funnel, he was able to drink along with the rest. To me, he was a fitting ambassador from the Argonne, representative of the million who went forward into that vast maze of caves and traps, of machine guns and cannon. My friend with the rubber tube and the swollen toes showed emotion only once, when he wept one night because he was unable to get to his feet and fight a brother officer from whom, he erroneously believed, he had suffered an insult.

The troops in the Argonne were not all of veteran caliber. Some divisions were relieved, but mainly they moved forward, halted at times by their own ineptitude, or by the sheer severity of the defense. They were humorists still. A carrier pigeon could arrive back at the pigeon wagons bearing the message: "I'm tired carrying this damned bird." The man who wrote that line was not far from the one in the Maine regiment that held the line at Gettysburg, a private who, when asked by his West Point colonel why he was chewing hardtack in the ranks, could reply: "For the juice, sir. I'm very fond of the juice."

A generation freshly memoried in the deeds of the Second World War cannot appreciate the simplicity of the first one. A brilliant defense at Château-Thierry, some fine bolstering counterattacks in the intervening two months before the reduction of Saint-Mihiel, and the great grinding sacrifices of the Argonne: that was the tale. It was told by correspondents still of the Richard Harding Davis tradition: it had no simple chroniclers such as Ernie Pyle. The result was that, when the men came home and began to write realistically of their experiences, the public was

shocked at literary and dramatic works that seem, at this far-off date, rather pale by contrast with the works that followed the later war. These were true shockers; but Pyle and his school of writing had prepared a public for them. A man will read of that first one, even in the most realistic postwar works that followed it, and have difficulty in capturing the simplicity of its mood. The gulf between the two, the abyss of sentiment, is simply unfathomable.

When the Armistice came on November 11, 1918, the victors gave their exultant cries and set out scrounging for *vin rouge;* but not so General Pershing. He had sent a regiment across the fire-raked pontoons of the Meuse the day before, for he wanted, like the boys in the song, to go to Berlin. Some years later he could say to a friend of mine, who was his officer of the guard on another occasion: "They don't know they were beaten in Berlin, and it will all have to be done all over again." The temper of his troops was such that they would have pressed forward at his word, as witness that regiment, with Armistice talk filling the air, fighting across the Meuse at Sedan.

In both wars there was, beyond the death and the mutilation, the heroism and sacrifice, an American feeling of idealism. The literature following the wake of both wars would deny this; writers try to single out the variation from the norm. The coward seems more interesting, in pedestrian literature, than the heroic figures chosen, say, by the Greeks in their great age. Even the films following the first war that were concerned with the gallantries of the aviators will show, on examination, that it is the boy who is frightened who holds the interest of the writer. It was a long while before Hemingway, in his *Farewell to Arms,* could examine a man who forsook the war, turning his back upon carnage, simply because he wanted no more of it. The play, *What Price Glory?* was attacked by many high-ranking officers; one of its authors was even subjected to the possibility of a court martial by President Coolidge; yet it could be said of its characters what Froissart said of the Plantagenets: "Whatever may have been their faults, there was not a coward among them."

One of the remarkable features of the Civil War was that, though peopled by great figures, it was followed by no great writing; only when Stephen Crane—a generation later, having never been near a battle himself—produced *The Red Badge of Courage,* were the men of its armies adequately pictured. In its way, the First World War left no great works either; some fine ones perhaps, but nothing like the work that Tolstoi, a generation after it, created from the wreck of Napoleon's dream; nothing like Stendhal's description of the field of Waterloo in *The Charterhouse of Parma*. Yet the men who returned from the first one were unhampered, uncensored; above all they were victorious. They could not set down, however, their deepest feelings about it, any more than could the men who shook hands at Appomattox. The best works of literature following the First World War were from the pens of men like Sinclair Lewis, who makes little mention of it, and Eugene O'Neill, who seems unaware of it. Both of them won the Nobel prize.

It may be a characteristic of the English-speaking races; for certainly the finest English work written during the period of the Napoleonic wars, when England was frequently on the ropes, is Miss Jane Austen's *Pride and Prejudice*. Written in an English garrison town, with one of its principals an officer in the army, it refers only on its last page to the war—or rather "the restoration of peace." And so it was with our war. There were no chroniclers, no painters, no writers reaching greatness because of it.

In Stendhal's account of Waterloo, in which he is actually adapting his own recollections as a French staff officer at Bautzen, where Ney failed to take an advantage and confusion followed, he restricts his field of vision to that enjoyed by a single green recruit. Actually, the men of Belleau Wood, of Saint-Mihiel, of the Argonne, saw little of their war, either.

The nature of the terrain, the squirrel-hunting tactics, made it impossible to get anything like a big picture of the scene. What could a platoon leader see of it? If he was knocked down and his face bloodied by a grenade, as he scrambled forward to regain his line he might see his own platoon; a flank of the one on the right wavering temporarily because its lieutenant was knocked down and dying; and beyond the line a few of the enemy heads sighting down the barrels of light machine guns. There were isolated instances of the panorama such as must have been vouchsafed Andrew Jackson's men at New Orleans, where behind mud ramparts the fog rose above meadowland full-dressed in British redcoats, echeloned and glinting as they moved forward toward the rifles of the Kentuckians and the Tennesseans.

Thomas Mann says somewhere that nothing is so remote, so difficult to recapture, as the immediate past. It must be that way with our First World War. The men who fought it are grandfathers, their own sons recalling a far more complex affair. And no anthologist can ever bring back the full body of it; though like all wars it carries thoughts too deep for tears.

Laurence Stallings, a marine veteran of two world wars, is the co-author of one of the most popular plays of the American stage, What Price Glory? *and the editor of a picture history of the First World War.*

Timid President? Futile War? CONTINUED FROM PAGE 47

result, many believed, would be a militia that could refuse to go onto foreign soil. Skeptically, Madison signed the bills for the regulars and the volunteers.

His skepticism had warrant. On June 8 the number of recruits was estimated at five thousand, and there were few unbalky volunteers except in the West.

With England unyielding, the President on March 31 notified the House Committee on Foreign Relations that he was ready to ask for a shipping embargo—a prelude to war. But "the Executive will not take upon itself the responsibility of declaring that we are prepared for war." Congress must make the final decision with its eyes open. Four days later it did so, the embargo taking effect on April 4.

By that time, military and naval decisions were crowding in upon the Executive. In those fields, two stories are told which carry the suggestion that Madison was stupid, or at least indecisive. The fact that they are still in circulation proves that some writers have been a trifle credulous. One story says that the

President decided to make an untrained civilian, Henry Clay, supreme military commander but was dissuaded by his Cabinet. The other is that Madison made up his mind to keep the American Navy tied up for harbor defense, but reversed himself on the pleas of Navy Captains Charles Stewart and William Bainbridge.

The story of the abortive appointment of Henry Clay reached full and rounded form in Calvin Colton's 1857 biography of Clay. It can be traced backward in print and manuscript, diminishing as it recedes—back to Colonel Isaac Cole's recollection, in 1838, of what he once heard from General John Mason, back to Mason's memory of what he was told by his brother-in-law, General Ben Howard. And that was: a group of Clay's friends suggested Clay's appointment to President Madison, who "assented to their opinion of [Clay's] fitness, etc., but said he could not be spared out of Congress." That was the molehill out of which the mountain grew.

The naval history was no third-hand, dry-land scuttlebutt. It came from Captain Stewart himself. As Stewart published the story in 1845, he and Captain Bainbridge went to the Navy Department on June 21, 1812, three days after the declaration of war, to solicit commands at sea. They were told by Secretary Paul Hamilton that the President and Cabinet had decided to keep the ships tied up. They protested, and the argument was continued before the President, who agreed with the captains but gave way to the Cabinet at a special meeting called that evening. Bainbridge and

James Madison

Stewart thereupon drafted a joint letter to the President, who overruled the Cabinet and ordered the Navy into action. Capping Stewart's story was his account of a great naval ball in the following December to which a courier brought news of Captain Stephen Decatur's victory over the frigate *Macedonian*. Whereupon President Madison told the assembled guests that if it had not been for Bainbridge and Stewart, the warships never would have gone to sea.

All rather convincing, unless you happen to know that Madison did not attend that December ball, that on June 23 Bainbridge wrote from Boston (he was not in Washington at all at the time) asking for a fighting command, and that all major warships ready for action were ordered to sea on the day war was declared. Stewart did not invent his 1845 story. It arose out of his muddled recollection and grandiose enlargement of a discussion held at the White House in February, 1812, some months before the declaration of war, in which the President sided with the captains against the Secretary of the Navy. Congress had just rejected the administration's request for twenty-two new warships. The captains, arguing with Hamilton, conceded that even if an American vessel were victorious it might, without reinforcements, be overwhelmed and captured by the enemy. To which Madison replied: "It is victories we want; if you give us them and lose your ships afterwards, they can be replaced by others."

The February discussion between the captains and the President was prophetic. For when Madison made his next request for greater sea power, in the closing weeks of 1812, it was dramatized by the *Constitution's* victory over the *Guerrière* in August, the capture of

the *Macedonian* by the *United States* in October, and especially by the gallant exploit of the sloop *Wasp*, which ran into exactly the kind of trouble Stewart and Bainbridge had predicted. Victorious over the *Frolic*, the *Wasp* was unable to hoist a sail when a lumbering British seventy-four came along and took both victor and prize to Bermuda. Captain Stewart, in this campaign for funds, furnished Secretary Hamilton with the technical arguments that helped persuade Congress to authorize four ships of the line, four heavy frigates, and as many sloops of war.

In one critical area the issue of naval power could not wait until the war began. In March, 1812, Stewart was called to Washington and offered a yet-uncreated command on the Great Lakes, controlled then by a few British armed vessels. The President intended to ask Congress for money to build a fleet; in the meantime enough would be scraped up for an eighteen-gun brig. Stewart refused; he was a deep-sea man.

The matter was given a new turn just then by Governor William Hull of Michigan Territory, a veteran of the Revolution. Offered a commission as brigadier general, he urged the building of lake squadrons. But with Stewart rejecting the command and Congress hostile to naval construction, Hull assured the President that he could lead an army across the Detroit River and down the north shore of Lake Erie to the Niagara River. That would restrain the northwestern Indians, deliver much of upper Canada into American hands, and win control of the lakes in less time and at less cost than the building of a fleet would require.

A Detroit campaign was being forced on the government anyway. Early operations against Montreal were made impossible by the dearth of regulars and the refusal of New England governors to furnish militia for federal service. On the other hand, western volunteers were so eager to break up the British-Indian alliance, Clay and others reported, that inaction might chill their spirit. Madison accepted Hull's promise of lake control by land action and thereby made the biggest strategic error of the war.

The appointment of Hull was a major blunder, but hardly a foreseeable one. Thirty years of peace with the Army almost nonexistent forced the President to choose his generals either from aging Revolutionary veterans with fighting experience and reputation, or from young regimental officers who had never seen action. Among the veterans called back, Hull had an unsurpassed Revolutionary record. Even Federalist editors applauded Madison's selection.

Hull commanded twenty-five hundred confident Kentuckians, Ohioans, regulars, and Michigan territorials. He crossed into Canada on July 12, 1812, skirmished with the vastly outnumbered enemy, and retreated to Fort Detroit. There, on August 16, without firing a shot, without consulting his officers, he surrendered his entire army to General Isaac Brock, who was advancing at the head of 330 British regulars and 400 Canadian militiamen, with several hundred Indians whooping in the woods.

Hull's claim that he was short of supplies was categorically denied by his officers but avidly accepted by the Federalist press, with a resultant impact on historians. His most startling assertion was that he had only one day's supply of powder. When he made the same remark to Sir George Prevost, the British commander handed him "the return of the large supply found in the fort; it did not create a blush." Those were the words of British Adjutant General Edward Baynes. Hull's actions, wrote another member of Prevost's staff, "stamp him either for a coward or a traitor." With such comments coming from the captors, it seems just a trifle severe to blame the surrender on either the President or the War Department.

Suppose, instead, we find out how the President reacted to the disaster. New land forces, he said, could be counted on to redeem the country's honor. The immediate necessity was to speed up the building of warships to gain control of the lakes—a method that would have been adopted at the outset "if the easy conquest of them by land held out to us [by Hull] had not misled our calculations." The strength of his feeling was recorded by Richard Rush, who wrote to John Adams the following June: "I know the President to be so convinced upon this subject that I heard him say last fall if the British build thirty frigates upon [the lakes] we ought to build forty."

Madison's insistence produced the warships with which Commodore Perry defeated and captured the British squadron on Lake Erie in September, 1813, changing the whole complexion of the war. He ordered the building of ship after ship on Lake Ontario. Superiority swung back and forth on that lake like reversing winds, but neither side could force a decision because each had protected bases—the British at York (now Toronto) and Kingston, the Americans at Sackets Harbor—to retire to when the other was ahead.

Far more important and more critical was the state of affairs in 1814 on Lake Champlain, the great sluice that opened a supply route northward to Montreal and southward to the Hudson River valley. By summer, more than twenty thousand seasoned veterans of the Peninsular War, released for transatlantic service by Napoleon's downfall, were crowding onto British transports bound for Canada, Chesapeake Bay, and New Orleans. On Lake Champlain, the American ship Saratoga was launched thirty-five days after the laying of

her keel. Sailors were in short supply both there and on Lake Ontario. Madison ordered the crews filled up with soldiers and told the protesting Secretary of War that naval efficiency was essential even for land operations.

Then came news that the enemy was building a new vessel on Lake Champlain, the Confiance, far more powerful than the twenty-six-gun Saratoga. Loss of the lake might still be averted, Captain Thomas Macdonough believed, by the swifter building of a light brig. Navy Secretary William Jones, though far more vigorous and capable than his predecessor, said the limit of available funds had been reached.

Madison ordered the ship built anyhow. Its keel had been laid when Jones again drew back. "God knows where the money is to come from," he wrote. The President reaffirmed the order and obtained a pledge of the utmost speed. On July 15 the timbers of the twenty-gun Eagle were still standing in the forest. The vessel was launched on August 11 and furnished the margin of power that changed sure defeat into a victory which resounded from Washington to Ghent.

"The battle of Lake Champlain, more than any other incident of the War of 1812, merits the epithet 'decisive,'" wrote the distinguished naval historian Alfred Thayer Mahan many years later. Within earshot of the battle, many of them within sight, nearly fourteen thousand of Wellington's battle-hardened soldiers waited for the Royal Navy to open the way to Albany and New York. When the British fleet surrendered, the army of invasion marched back to Canada and never returned.

In naval affairs, Madison could rely on officers unsurpassed anywhere in the world for knowledge and ability. In army matters he had to learn by hard experience. His first Secretary of War, William Eustis, was a Massachusetts medical man of bustling energy who bore a tremendous load of work in a War Department consisting of himself and eight clerks. Eustis, even in the opinion of some congressmen who wanted him fired, outperformed what anybody had a right to expect in equipping the Army as war approached. But he had no more than a civilian's knowledge of military operations, did little to systematize the nation's defenses, and seemed unable to recognize incompetence in field officers before it was demonstrated in battle. The President shared this last fault. When Adjutant General Baynes visited Major General Henry Dearborn under a flag of truce, he saw at a glance that the American commander lacked energy. Neither Madison nor Eustis sensed this, and the President couldn't see the deficiencies of Eustis. His resignation, after failures on the Niagara front followed the Hull catastrophe, was a concession to public opinion.

Brigadier General John Armstrong, who succeeded Eustis, was notorious for political intrigue but had enough of a military reputation to warrant his selection. The President chose him reluctantly, after Secretary of State James Monroe and Senator William Harris Crawford had refused the place.

During the next year and a half, until the burning of Washington forced him to resign, Armstrong performed his work with one eye on the war and the other on the 1816 presidential race. His good and bad traits showed up at once but not in equal measure. He drove the competent Andrew Jackson to fury and disobedience with a brusque, unappreciative dismissal of his temporary Tennessee volunteers in a distant wilderness. He removed the incompetent General Dearborn with a note even more callous. Both men wrote to the President, Jackson boiling with indignation, Dearborn heartbroken. Madison forced Armstrong to make amends to Jackson. He himself consoled Dearborn but affirmed the removal.

Armstrong's strategy to gain the presidential nomination paralleled that of his rival, James Monroe. Each hoped to be made a lieutenant general and win the war. Monroe's chance vanished when Armstrong took the War Department. Armstrong's opportunity seemed to open when the President, in June of 1813, was stricken with an almost fatal illness followed by several months' convalescence in Virginia. Freed of effective presidential supervision, Armstrong went north under the pretense of making an inspection trip and did not come back until Christmas. During the interval he assumed personal direction of a two-pronged campaign against Montreal, failed to co-ordinate the mishandled offensive movements, and ducked away to Albany to watch the approaching double fiasco as a detached observer.

Personal ambition and laziness turned Armstrong's strategic ideas, even when sound, into flashy gambits, without the preparation or drive required to follow through. Two weeks before the event that drove him out of office, he received a written rebuke from Madison that would have pierced the hide of a rhinoceros—though it did not penetrate his—for secretly exercising powers delegated by Congress to the President, ordering military operations without consultation, suppressing letters intended for the President, accepting the resignation of General William Henry Harrison without authority, and posing to Harrison's successor as the bestower of the appointment.

Nevertheless, Armstrong possessed capabilities that, combined with Madison's ability to thwart their misuse, gave a new look to the American Army. Both men recognized youthful talent, and Armstrong was ruthless enough to get rid of old incompetents.

Zebulon Pike, promoted to brigadier general, was killed in winning his first victory. Jacob Brown and George Izard, lately raised to the same rank, stood out in the Montreal campaign in contrast to their soon-to-be-ousted commanders, Major Generals James Wilkinson and Wade Hampton. Shining talents were displayed by Colonels E. P. Gaines and Winfield Scott; solid performance by Alexander Macomb, T. A. Smith, E. W. Ripley. Every one of these eight men was recommended by Armstrong for promotion, with the exception of Brown. He advised the President that for major generals, not a moment should be lost in promoting Brigadiers Izard and Thomas Flournoy.

Flournoy, a nobody at New Orleans! His promotion, by making Andrew Jackson his subordinate instead of his superior, would have knocked Jackson straight out of the military service—if not into apoplexy. But it also would have barricaded the upward path of Brown —the man most likely to stand in Armstrong's way if Armstrong succeeded in establishing the grade of lieutenant general—by filling all the major-generalships allowed by law.

The President nominated Izard—*and Brown*. It could almost be said that at that moment the Battle of New Orleans was won, although Jackson's appointment as major general still awaited a future vacancy. Also, the leadership was established that retrieved American prestige in the 1814 battles of the Niagara peninsula and helped persuade England that the time was ripe for peace.

The location of that Niagara campaign, illogical because of its limited objective, resulted from troop movements made by Armstrong without consulting the President. To remedy that feature, the Secretary sent a proposal to Madison at Montpelier that Brown's army bypass the peninsula and swing around Lake Ontario to Burlington and York. Madison imposed the same restriction that was to be recognized a hundred years later by Admiral Mahan: control of the lake must first be won to prevent the landing of an army in the American rear. The civilian commander in chief was learning the art of war. By a succession of decisions affecting strength, strategy, and leadership on Lake Champlain, at New Orleans, and on the Niagara front —overruling his subordinates in every instance—Madison went far to determine the outcome.

In spite of their conflicts over appointments, Armstrong and the President worked effectively together in a fundamental regeneration of the military command. On the day war was declared the United States Army had eight generals, most of them just appointed. Their average age was sixty years. Two years later all of them were out of service or assigned to quiescence. In the first half of 1814 nine generals were appointed or promoted—their average age was thirty-six—and these men turned raw American recruits into disciplined soldiers. When the war ended they had just begun to fight.

These redeeming events of 1814 are obscured in popular narrative and even in histories by the burning of Washington and the miserable failure of its defenders. (*See* "The Day They Burned the Capitol," AMERICAN HERITAGE, December, 1954.) For that occurrence President Madison bore an inescapable responsibility: constitutionally, he was commander in chief; physically, he was in Washington when the enemy approached. Why did he not foresee the attack, or, if he did, why didn't he guard against it?

The answer to the first question accentuates the second. On May 24, after reading a British proclamation calling for a general uprising of southern slaves, the President wrote to Armstrong that this presaged a campaign of ruthless devastation in which the national capital could not fail to be "a favorite target." On July 1, without dissent but with skepticism concerning the danger (so wrote Navy Secretary William Jones), the Cabinet approved Madison's proposal that ten thousand militiamen be drawn out to help guard the Washington-Baltimore area. When Brigadier General William H. Winder wished to summon them, Secretary Armstrong (the chief skeptic) made the fatal reply that the best mode of using militia "was upon the spur of the occasion." Nevertheless, the power and responsibility belonged to the President, and his own recorded foresight called for vigorous defensive measures. He intervened again and again, to overcome Armstrong's sloth and skepticism, but never forced action on a large enough scale.

Almost in another world is the popular word-picture of the Madisons at this time. It is a composite of Dolley saving the portrait of George Washington as the enemy approached, and of the President—as depicted by the scurrilous (and anonymous) versifier of "The Bladensburg Races"—galloping in terrified flight forty miles into Maryland.

The rhapsodic glee with which the versifier danced in the ashes of the Capitol and White House may not impeach his veracity, but his figurative observation post hardly matched the physical one of Sérurier, who had a panoramic view from the unmenaced Octagon House. The President, Sérurier wrote to Talleyrand two days before the battle, "has just gone to the camp to encourage, by his presence, the army to defend the capital." Madison returned to the White House from the actual battlefield (where Congreve rockets fell near him) after Dolley left the house. He remained there, the French minister said, until after the Georgetown and Washington militia streamed by in confused flight

toward Frederick. The manner of his departure as described by Sérurier would be of little moment except that it emphasizes still further how different Madison's character was from the one history has bestowed on him:

It was then, my lord, that the President, who, in the midst of all this disorder, had displayed to stop it a firmness and constancy worthy of a better success . . . coolly mounted his horse, accompanied by some friends, and slowly gained the bridge that separates Washington from Virginia.

By the time the news of the burning of Washington reached London, the bellicosity and bad temper that had given rise to Admiral Alexander Cochrane's "treat 'em rough" instructions were things of the past. War weariness in England, fresh dangers emerging in chaotic Europe, and the sharp improvement in the American position, strength, and morale in the north, all helped produce a sudden reversal of British policy at Ghent. Peace was signed the day before Christmas, and the fighting ended on January 8, 1815, when two thousand British soldiers—a third of the entire assaulting army—fell dead or wounded at New Orleans.

The Treaty of Ghent left things as they were. Did the war itself leave them unchanged? Impressment and the Orders in Council both vanished before the treaty was signed. European peace removed them as immediate future hazards. If the war had lifted American prestige, no treaty was needed to abolish them forever. By that measurement the New Orleans victory was climax, not epilogue. In 1815, Justice Joseph Story weighed the results of the war and found them massive:

Never did a country occupy more lofty ground; we have stood the contest, single-handed, against the conqueror of Europe; and we are at peace, with all our blushing victories thick crowding on us. If I do not much mistake, we shall attain to a very high character abroad as well as crush domestic faction.

Domestic faction was crushed in the next election. Those who would fix the time at which the country attained international stature might ask themselves: Could there have been a Monroe Doctrine in 1823 without the War of 1812? It was under the quiet guiding hand of President James Madison that the struggling young republic won an equal position among the free nations of the world, and began its long climb to leadership.

Irving Brant, journalist and historian, has been an editorial writer for newspapers in St. Louis and Chicago. He is the author of, among many other books, a multivolume biography of President Madison.

LIBERTY

COTTON

Behold the man ! He said that COTTON
Would surely make them inde-*pendant!*
But see, my friend, "the *string* he's got on,"
A fit adornment to the end on't.

UNCLE
SAM
JEFF
DAVIS
HIS MARK

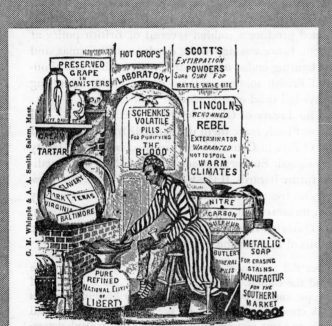

G. M. Whipple & A. A. Smith, Salem, Mass.

HOT DROPS

SCOTT'S
EXTIRPATION
POWDERS
SURE CURE FOR
RATTLE SNAKE BITE

PRESERVED
GRAPE
IN
CANISTERS

LABORATORY

CREAM
TARTAR

SCHENKL'S
VOLATILE
PILLS
For Purifying
THE
BLOOD

LINCOLN'S
RENOWNED
REBEL
EXTERMINATOR
WARRANTED
NOT TO SPOIL IN
WARM
CLIMATES

SLAVERY
DARK TEXAS
VIRGINIA
BALTIMORE

NITRE
CARBON
SULPHUR

BUTLER'S
MINERAL
PILLS

METALLIC
SOAP
FOR ERASING
STAINS:
MANUFACTUR
FOR THE
SOUTHERN
MARKET

PURE
REFINED
NATIONAL ELIXIR
OF
LIBERTY

A MORAL

Spirit of the South.

Around the year 1850, some ingenious American printer originated the idea of the "Patriotic Envelope." Symbols and emblems in one or two colors were printed on the left side of the envelopes—usually the American flag, figures symbolizing Unity and Happiness, the Eagle, or a group of soldiers.

Slowly a change took place; the quaint and idyllic gave way to aggressive political caricature. Inevitably, presidential elections provided the occasion for many spirited demonstrations of political parti-

Agricultural Implements going South.

"DEATH BEFORE DISHONOR."

I'SE CONTRABAND.

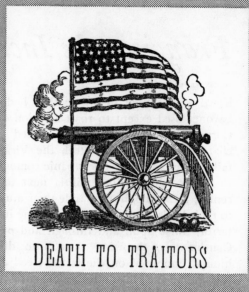

DEATH TO TRAITORS

N THE MAIL

sanship, and with the coming of the Civil War the patriotic envelope came into its heyday. North and South swamped each other with this early effort at psychological warfare. On thousands of envelopes there poured out a flood of persiflage and patriotic sentiment, contrasting the highest national ideals with the low and treacherous aims of the adversary.

Some of these envelopes have great artistic value; others can charitably be defined as valuable documents of a folk art that has seldom been practiced since. The envelopes themselves have long been rare items. These examples are from the collection, probably the finest in the country, of Dr. N. T. Gidal.

"WE HAVE NAILED OUR COLORS TO THE MAST."

Francisco the Incredible

CONTINUED FROM PAGE 25

heard a shot fired in anger; they had never seen a bayonet used except to roast a ration of beef. When Cornwallis' seasoned regulars loosed a volley and charged with gleaming steel, the Virginians turned tail, broke, and ran. Their panic communicated itself to the North Carolina militia next to them in the center; these, too, hurled aside their muskets and took to their heels. Some 2,500 men, fleeing in uncontrolled terror, burst upon and through and over the sturdy Continentals, throwing them into disorder. Gates himself, mounted on the fastest steed available, won the race to the rear and did not pause in his frenzied gallop until he had put many miles between himself and the enemy.

On a day when the commanding general flies the white feather so conspicuously, the man of courage who stands and fights looms larger than life-size by contrast. All around Peter Francisco were wildly running, screaming men. Abandoned in the melee was a small field piece, one of two that had been wheeled into line between the Virginia and North Carolina militia; now it was about to be seized by the enemy.

Peter Francisco saw the cannon and acted. According to the legend, he ran to the gun, stooped, strained his mighty smith's muscles until they almost snapped— then straightened and lifted the 1,100-pound cannon on his back! Bowed under more than half a ton of iron, he staggered off to the rear, found a knot of Continentals still standing firm, and delivered his burden.

Even legend agrees that Peter Francisco was badly spent after this exploit. His own unit had been scattered like dust before a tornado; there was no duty for him to perform; and so he went into the woods to rest. He had hardly regained his breath when one of Tarleton's hard-charging troopers burst through the scattered pines and reared above him, prepared to cut him down at the first hostile gesture.

The trooper offered Francisco two choices: surrender or death. Protesting that his musket was empty, the American lifted it up and extended it sidewise, stretching it out to the trooper in a mute gesture of surrender. The cavalryman fell for the ruse and reached for the gun. As he did, Francisco twirled it lightning-fast in his hands and thrust viciously with the same motion. The bayonet speared the incautious trooper through the body and pitched him, dying, from the saddle. As he tumbled, Francisco leaped upon the horse and rode off through the woods.

He had not gone far when he found Tarleton's men all around him. Rising in the stirrups, he impersonated a deliriously happy Tory. "Huzzah, my brave boys," he cried out, "we've conquered the rebels!" And so, shouting and cheering, he passed through the troop and up the road to safety.

Suddenly he saw his regimental commander, Colonel Mayo, trudging along on foot, the prisoner of a British officer. Francisco, charging up on horseback, cut down the officer and freed Mayo. Then, alighting from the horse, he insisted that the Colonel take it and ride to safety. Reluctantly the Colonel agreed, and Francisco relied on his own giant strides to escape.

It is here that modern skeptics, trying to sift truth from fiction in the Francisco legend, come upon one of those undeniable kernels of fact that seems to say that all, incredible as it may seem, is true. Francisco's deed in lugging the 1,100-pound cannon from the battlefield is part of the legend. It was a story always told in his lifetime, widely believed, apparently never challenged. About the rescue of Colonel Mayo, it appears there can be no doubt at all.

The Colonel himself never forgot Francisco's generosity in insisting that he take the captured horse and escape. Years later, after the war, he presented Francisco with the small dress sword he had always worn on formal occasions, and still later, in his will, he bequeathed to Francisco one thousand acres of Kentucky land. The Mayo heirs protested this provision of the will, and Francisco, too proud to battle the case in court, never did receive the bequest. But he treasured the dress sword all his life, and it is still preserved at the Virginia Historical Society in Richmond.

Back in Virginia after the disaster of Camden, a cavalry troop was being formed under a Captain Watkins in Prince Edward County, and Francisco took the huge, five-foot broadsword given him by George Washington, supplied himself with a good horse, and joined up. His troop soon left for the embattled Carolinas, where the Americans at last had found a real commander, Major General Nathanael Greene.

Attempting to repair the wreckage left by Gates, Greene was parrying and fencing with Cornwallis, keeping just out of reach while he built up his army, when Watkins' cavalry troop joined Greene's light dragoons, under the command of Colonel William Washington. Once his little army was ready for action, Greene returned to North Carolina and a battle site he had picked out long before. This was Guilford Courthouse, and here, on March 15, 1781, the Americans and British collided in one of the bloodiest battles of the war, one that virtually determined the fate of the southern colonies.

Greene drew up his army in three lines. The third line, the heart of his position, was on a cleared crest of steeply rising ground surrounding the courthouse. To attack it, the British would have to advance upward along a snaking road that led through a wooded defile, across a clearing ringed by woods, and then through more woods up to the open slope about the courthouse. The woods made ideal cover for sharpshooting riflemen, and the ground sloped upward from the road on both sides, giving the Americans hidden on the flanks a chance to pour a deadly fire down upon the files of the advancing enemy.

In the bright sunshine of early afternoon, with the air crisp, Cornwallis approached through the wooded defiles to challenge Greene on Greene's chosen ground. As the British moved up the road through the woods, formed at the edge of the little clearing, and then started moving across it, the first and second American lines gave a good account of themselves; Lynch's Virginia riflemen and Kirkwood's light infantry even launched a counterattack that broke the British ranks and drove them down the slope in great disorder. But the enemy re-formed and came back for more. Lieutenant Colonel Stuart rallied a crack regiment of British guardsmen, took other troops from the battle with the Virginia militia on the American left, and hurled the whole force up the slope at the last line, piercing the very heart of Greene's front.

In this moment of triumph, the redcoats swept forward shouting, the day all but won. Just as they did, off on the right wing, William Washington and his cavalry changed everything with one mighty stroke. Ordering his bugler to sound the charge, Washington launched his troopers straight down the slope in a thundering assault on Stuart's flank and rear. In the van, a massive figure wielding his tremendous broadsword, rode Peter Francisco.

The shock as the cavalry crashed into the exposed enemy ranks resounded over the battlefield. The momentum of the charge swept all before it. Washington's cavalry rode roughshod over the guardsmen, then wheeled and headed back, literally hacking the British regiment to pieces.

Especially terrifying was the gigantic figure of Peter Francisco. Man after man went down before the overpowering strokes of his broadsword. Legend has it that, possessed by the frenzy of battle, he delivered one blow with such superhuman force that it split a guardsman's body in half down the column of the backbone. Eleven men in a row fell before him. Describing his feat, Benson J. Lossing, the early authority on the Revolution, told how one of the guardsmen finally

"pinned Francisco's leg to his horse with a bayonet. Forbearing to strike, he [Francisco] assisted the assailant to draw his bayonet forth, when, with terrible force, he brought down his broadsword and cleft the poor fellow's head to his shoulders! Horrible indeed were many of the events of that battle, the recital will do no good, and I will forbear."

Even the leg wound, his fourth of the war, did not take Francisco out of the fight. The issue had not yet been decided; more remained to be done. The Continental infantry, plunging down the slope of the courthouse hill, rushed into the bloody breach Washington's troops had carved, putting the stunned guardsmen to the bayonet. Cornwallis, seeing the massacre, rushed up the road in person to relieve his menaced army. He was protected only by a thin screen of troopers, and William Washington, alert to the opportunity, yelled to Francisco and others and led a charge on the British ranks in the hope of capturing the General.

Cornwallis quickly drew back, his troops forming a protective screen around him. Washington, foiled, drew off and led his cavalry in one final assault on the rear ranks of the shattered redcoats. Seasoned troops, they had recovered slightly from the first shock and were forming in squares. In this last melee, Peter Francisco received another and almost mortal wound.

Riding headlong upon the solidifying squares of the guardsmen, he was impaled upon a bayonet upthrust from the sturdy, prickly hedge. The steel entered his leg just above the knee, sliced deep almost to the bone and ripped upward, laying open the flesh along the entire upper leg almost to the hip socket. Nearly unhorsed by the shock, doubled up with pain, Francisco wheeled out of the action, clung to his mount in desperation, and then, losing consciousness, tumbled from the saddle and collapsed on the battleground.

Behind him the bayonet-wielding Continentals, seizing the opportunity the cavalry had given them, were tearing to shreds the entire center of the British army. Cornwallis had to stop the carnage or lose everything. To the horror of his officers, he wheeled forward his artillery, ordered the gunners to load with grape and train their muzzles directly on the melee in the center, where his own men were mixed inextricably with the charging Americans. General O'Hara, who had been wounded earlier in the action and was lying by the side of the road, could see what his commander planned to do, and was horrified.

Lafayette, young hero of the Revolution, revisited America in 1824 and received a warm welcome at Castle Garden in New York City. Peter Francisco, who had met the Marquis at the Battle of Brandywine, toured Virginia with him.

"Stop, stop," he pleaded, "you will destroy your own men."

"We must do it to save ourselves from destruction," Cornwallis answered.

And he ordered the guns to fire. They roared out, and Cornwallis, iron-faced, stood there watching his own guns slaughter his own troops in order to halt the enemy. The inhuman strategy worked. The deadly grapeshot scythed through the ranks of friend and foe and stilled the milling fury of the battle. Under the steady hammering of the guns, the Americans withdrew slowly and reluctantly to their own lines; the British fell back spent, trying to re-form.

This was virtually the end of the battle. Greene had the only army in being in the south; he was in no position to risk total destruction on the chance of total victory. Reluctantly, he drew off in good order, fighting a rear-guard action as he went. Cornwallis, technically the victor, rested on the field that had witnessed the virtual destruction of his army as a fighting force. He had suffered losses he could not afford to suffer; he had paid so high a price for victory that never again could he dominate the south. Ahead lay the last long march into Virginia—and Yorktown.

As for Peter Francisco, he lay on the battlefield still as the dead. A Quaker named Robinson, searching the field to see if any were alive, found him still breathing, took him home, and slowly nursed him back to health.

While the young giant was recuperating, the story of his incredible performance on the bloody field of Guilford Courthouse became the talk of the southern

army. None who fought there that day, apparently, ever forgot the huge soldier with the terrible sword. William Washington was so impressed that he urged Francisco to accept a commission, but the latter declined, feeling unqualified because he could neither read nor write. Nathanael Greene expressed his admiration by having a handsome razor case especially made for the hero. On it was inscribed: "Peter Francisco, New Store, Buckingham County, Va. A tribute to his moral worth and valor. From his comrade in Arms Nathanael Greene." The razor case still exists, preserved in the museum at Guilford Courthouse National Military Park, Greensboro, North Carolina. And on the battlefield itself a monument commemorates Francisco's spectacular feat.

By the time Francisco had recovered from the leg-splitting bayonet thrust that had almost cost him his life, the war had moved ahead of him. Cornwallis had taken his badly shattered army to Wilmington, North Carolina, and from there north to unite with a smaller British army that had been ravaging Virginia. By the time Francisco was well enough to travel, the heart of the southern war had moved into his home state, and the stage was being set for Yorktown.

Trudging north on foot, Francisco immediately volunteered his services and began to scout the countryside, then controlled by the roving troopers of Banastre Tarleton and other British raiders. It was a risky service. One day, while Francisco was stopping at Ward's Tavern in what is now Nottoway County, nine of Tarleton's dragoons burst up the road at a gallop, surprising and surrounding him in the inn yard. It was useless to resist, and Francisco stood quietly, like a man submitting to his fate.

Most of the troopers went inside the tavern, but one, saber drawn, approached Francisco. The conversation, as Alexander Garden later related it, perhaps with an embellishment or two of his own, went like this:

"Give up instantly and surrender everything you have of value—or prepare to die!" the trooper thundered.

"I have nothing to give up," said Francisco, with a shrug. "So use your pleasure."

The dragoon's covetous eyes were drawn to a pair of large silver buckles, a gift of Judge Winston, on Francisco's shoes.

"Give me instantly those silver buckles on your shoes," the cavalryman ordered, waving his sword.

"They were a present to me from a valued friend," Francisco protested. "Give them into your hands, I never will. You have the power. Take them if you think fit."

The dragoon decided to act on the invitation. He tucked his saber beneath his arm and stooped to snatch the buckles. As he did so the saber, hilt first, came within Francisco's reach. He grasped the hilt, wrenched the saber free, and in almost the same sweeping motion delivered an awesome stroke, splitting the trooper's head and neck in half down to his shoulders.

Instantly all was confusion—such confusion that the details of what happened next are indistinct. As nearly as the picture can be pieced together now, this was approximately the sequence.

The sabering of the dragoon brought the rest of Tarleton's troop rushing from the tavern. One aimed a pistol at Francisco. Francisco sprang at him with the saber. The dragoon fired even as the saber fell. The ball grazed Francisco's side—his sixth wound—but his own blow practically severed the hand that had fired the shot, and with another, Francisco cut the trooper down.

While he was doing this, another of the dragoons leaped to horse. Ben Ward, the tavern keeper, who had come running into the yard with the dragoons, chose this minute to cast his lot with what he fancied must prove the winning side. He grabbed a musket and passed it up to the mounted dragoon.

The trooper leveled the gun at Francisco's breast and pulled the trigger. It missed fire. Immediately, Francisco was upon him. Reaching up, he grabbed the musket, wrenched it from the dragoon's hands, clubbed him from the saddle, and sprang upon the horse, acquiring a post of vantage above his enemies.

He rose in the stirrups and hallooed, just as if he were really at the head of a thundering troop: "Come on, my brave boys, now's your time; let's dispatch these few!" At once he charged, cutting down another dragoon in the inn yard. The rest of the squad broke and fled, running in panic across the fields in all directions.

But the rest of Tarleton's troop, some four hundred men, had come into view in the distance, riding toward the tavern. Seeing the disturbance, ten of them broke out in front of the rest, riding to cut off Francisco. He tarried no longer. Putting spurs to his captured horse, he took off down an obscure country road and with his knowledge of the countryside easily eluded his pursuers.

The skirmish at Ward's Tavern was the last of Francisco's wartime exploits. He was in the lines at Yorktown when Cornwallis surrendered, but after this climactic victory, he turned his thoughts to other pursuits—specifically, to a girl, Susannah Anderson, whom he married in 1785.

With marriage, prosperity came to Peter Francisco.

Susannah apparently brought him the estate, Locust Grove, at which they lived; he acquired more slaves and property and became a planter and country gentleman. He read avidly in ancient and modern history, treating his books as carefully as treasures, and began to exhibit a taste for high hats, silk stockings, and bright waistcoats.

Yet he did not become a parlor effete. When any deed of seemingly superhuman strength was to be performed, Peter Francisco always seemed equal to the challenge. Once, the story goes, a milch cow and her calf had become stuck in the mud. Francisco picked up the cow under one arm, the calf under the other, and carried both to firm ground. Another time, on a muddy highway in winter, he came upon a heavily laden wagon stalled in the mire. Telling the driver to unhitch the mules, Francisco put his shoulders against the rear of the wagon, heaved, and lifted it clear.

In 1824, when Lafayette revisited America, the two Revolutionary warriors were reunited, and Francisco accompanied the Marquis on his triumphal tour through Virginia. Two years later, Henry Clay came to see Francisco and was much impressed by his host's still-mighty muscles.

In such fashion, with strength and vigor almost undiminished, did Peter Francisco live to the end of his days. He was widowed twice, but each time remarried. Then, in 1831, he himself became ill—of an intestinal ailment that physicians in a wiser era might have diagnosed as appendicitis. He suffered for three weeks before he died at an age estimated as seventy. Lafayette, when notified of his death, was deeply affected and sent a letter of sympathy to Francisco's widow. The Virginia legislature passed a resolution of regret, and state officials from the governor down attended the funeral service held in the General Assembly Hall.

Despite his almost incredible exploits, Peter Francisco has remained a hero virtually unknown in modern times. Yet he has not been altogether forgotten. Just before the turn of the present century, the Daughters of the American Revolution planted in San Francisco's Golden Gate Park thirteen "liberty trees," one for each of the original colonies, each tree nourished by soil taken from the grave of a Revolutionary hero. Virginia's symbol was the chestnut, and the earth around its base came from the grave of Peter Francisco.

Fred J. Cook, of the staff of the New York World-Telegram and Sun, *contributed "Allan McLane, Unknown Hero of the Revolution," to the October, 1956, issue of* AMERICAN HERITAGE *and "The Slave Ship Rebellion" in February, 1957. This article is adapted from Mr. Cook's new book,* What Manner of Man, *published by William Morrow.*

"*I have supped full on horrors*" CONTINUED FROM PAGE 65

6 P.M.—accompanied by Mary Titus, who is to stop at Yonkers. Early in the evening the President, who returned from City Point in the afternoon) was here. When I went into the room he was lying on the foot of Father's bed, talking with him. I said good evening, & was passing around to my seat on the other side, when I saw a long arm extended back around the foot of the bed, to shake hands in his cordial way. He stayed some time—told us Mʳ Stanton had told him he gave father up at first. He told us much about his visit to Richmond, & that one of his last acts was going through a hospital of seven thousand men, & shaking hands with each one. He spoke of having worked as hard at it as sawing wood—& seemed, in his goodness of heart, much satisfied at the labor. He spoke of the escort that met him & took him into Richmond—& his son Robert with them. (It was the last time I ever saw our beloved President—kind, genial & unaffected—he lay talking to Father on his sick bed, & after perhaps an hour—rose, & went from our sight forever.) Later in the evening Mʳ Stanton came & told Father that at *4 o'c today Gen Lee surrendered himself and his army to General Grant.* "God be praised!" said Father. Mʳ Stanton then related the particulars of the event. Such news is unspeakbly thrilling & momentous.

Monday April 10ᵗʰ Father felt better—had his arm & jaw bandaged early—sat up twice during the day. The doctors were all here at once this morning—besides coming separately during the day. Clarence was here in the morning, & left town during the day. Mother was better. The streets were in jubilee over the glorious news from Grant. All department employees had a holiday. The streets were filled with happy people, marching about with flags and bands of music. Mother & I watched them from the windows of Father's room. Besides the salutes fired by order of Mʳ Stanton, some people from the Navy Yard carried about two howitzers—firing them.

Recᵈ letters from Mʳˢ Perry [8] & Crissie K. Seward. [9]

Tuesday April 11ᵗʰ Though I believe there were no unfavorable symptoms, Father did not seem so well today. Once while I was with Father I began to read to him "Enoch Arden"—but the papers came soon after, & Fred read them to him.

The public buildings were illuminated in the evening, in honor of the news of Sunday. We could see the State Department, looking very finely, from our

windows—also—less distinctly, the President's house. There were three bands in the neighbor-hood—one at the State Dept. A transparency was used at the State Department, which father had prepared for an illumination in 1861, which did not take place (on account of Willie Lincoln's death) The words were "The Union saved by fidelity to the Constitution, Faith in the People, & Trust in God."

Wednsday April 12ᵗʰ Father had a bad night, but seemed better during the day— The physicians think favorably of his condition. They were each here three times today. In the morning, in place of bandaging, Dʳ Norris secured the fractured jaw by a wire from one tooth to the other. The operation was less painful than we apprehended, & the arrangement much more comfortable than the bandaging. His suffering today was augmented by gout in the right foot—but it is considered a good thing to divert a tendency to inflammation. Before 10 o'c—(when I retired) Dʳ Norris gave him a medecine (valerian & something else) to produce calm sleep, which he much needed. We thought he would have a very quiet night.

Thursday April 13ᵗʰ The medecine did not have the anticipated effect. Father had a very uncomfortable night—the medecine & the inflammation of the foot together made him delerious. He was still confused when morning came. He wanted to see Mʳ Harrington [10]—who was sent for very early, & coming, soothed him by passing his hand over his brow. During the morning Anna and I were with him—alternately or together. Mother had been up with him, also Fred. He sat up a long time. Anna read him the papers. Dʳ Barnes was here twice, Dʳ Norris morning, afternoon, and evening, Dʳ Verdi 3 or 4 times. Evening, Mʳ Stanton was here. Lynchburg is ours. There was a grand illumination of the city—public buildings & private residences, this evening. Owing to Father's illness we did not illuminate. There were superb fire works in La Fayette square. Mother & I watched them from the window of Father's room. Some of them were like bursting shells—and a new hospital nurse who comes to assist in taking care of Father at night, George Robinson,[11] told us the fireworks were quite a good representation of a skirmish fire such as he was

---

8 Mother of two of Fanny's closest friends in Auburn.
9 Christiana Frederika Kimbler, who married Fanny's cousin Samuel Swayze Seward.

10 George Harrington, the Assistant Secretary of the Treasury and 1865–1869 minister to Switzerland.
11 Sergeant George F. Robinson, a convalescent soldier assigned to the Sewards as a nurse. He and Augustus Seward were the prosecution's key witnesses in the trial and conviction of Lewis Payne.

used to. The signal lights, red, yellow & green were very beautiful. Mother & I enjoyed the sight very much. I remember how bright & cheerful she was. Dᵣ Norris came— He told me a little about the illumination of the city. Father seemed better in the afternoon. Dᵣ Norris came in the night to see him.

Good Friday. April 14ᵗʰ 1865. Father had a better night than any of late, and seemed the better after his refreshing sleep— He took solid food for the first time since his accident—breakfasted on soft egg, milk-toast, shad and coffee. Today a distinguished party perform the ceremony of raising the flag on Fort Sumter, taken from us 4 years ago.

So far I had written in pencil, in my pocket diary on the day of the date— I think I remember beginning the page, & wondering if I should have anything unsual to enter there later in the day. The rest of the page is filled with out-lines of what occurred later— from which, & from a longer account written three weeks later at my earliest leisure—(to relieve my mind of its weight of recollection) I write the following account. I can only give my remembrances, which are very vivid in my own mind—but I cannot describe all that took place, because in many instances I cannot remember to have seen some who were in the room— Anna, for instance—& Robinson part of the time.

First we had a quiet afternoon. Father so much better that he told Donaldson [12] he need not stay— I sat alone with him some time and read "Enoch Arden" to him. He spoke very highly of it. In the evening a torch-light procession of employees from the Navy Yard or Arsenal, visited the White House. I think it was earlier than that, that I was some time with Mother, in our room—part of the time she was lying down. I was telling her how any recital of suffering affected & haunted me—and she told me it had always been so with her. I think we talked much together— Anna & I watched the procession, & listened to the music—they played "Rally Round the Flag," & were singing too I believe, as they approached the White House. I came to my room to show Anna a book of soldier's songs, in which was the "Year of Jubilee," of which I had been telling her. Mother & she & I talked a little there— Then came the quiet arrangements for the night, in father's room— Fred & Anna & Mother had been up a great deal— That evening it was arranged that Gus should rest till 11—then sit up till in the night when Donaldson would come— Meantime I was to have the watch while Gus rested, & Robinson was to be there till George, the german nurse, relieved him. I sat by the side of the bed nearest the door, reading "Legends of Charlemagne," Robinson was

12 James Donaldson, State Department clerk and messenger.

near. I saw that Father seemed inclined to sleep—so turned down the gas, laid my book on a stand at the foot of the bed, & took a seat on the other side. About 10 o'c—Dᵣ Norris paid his visit—& left us all quiet. Father fell into a light sleep. Fred came in at the door, & glancing at the bed, saw his father slept, and said he would come in again. After he had gone, Father opened his eyes with a little smile of recognition as he saw me at the foot of the bed. He was lying close on the edge, farthest from the door— I do not remember hearing voices outside, but something led me to think that Fred was there with someone else. It occurred to me that he might have some important reason for wishing to see Father awake. Perhaps the President was there, or had sent over. I did not stop to see if father wakened thoroughly, but hastened to the door, opened it a very little, and found Fred standing close by it, facing me. On his right hand, also close by the door, stood a very tall young man, in a light hat & long overcoat. I said "Fred, Father is awake now." Something in Fred's manner led me at once to think that he did not wish me to say so, and that I had better not have opened the door. This confused me, & looking around I was glad to see Father going to sleep again. Holding the door as I did, I know the man could not see my father at all, nor could Fred, I think. I do not remember what Fred said to me. The man seemed impatient, & addressing me in a tone that struck me at once as much more harsh & full

When Secretary of War Stanton got word of the murder attempt, he rushed to Seward's bedside.

of determination than such a simple question justified, asked "Is the Secretary asleep." I paused to look at my father, & replied "Almost." Then Fred drew the door shut very quickly. I sat down again. I had no means of telling the errand of the man. I fancied some one had sent him—that he was, perhaps, a messenger from the telegraph office. Very soon I heard the sound of blows —it seemed to me as many as half a dozen—sharp and heavy, with lighter one's between. There had been an interval of quiet. I did not fully connect this with the person I had seen. I thought they were chasing a rat in the hall, remembering such a chase once. But when the blows continued, I could not tell what it meant, & said to Robinson, who was sitting at the head of the bed, on the side nearest the door, "What can be the matter? Do go and see." Then I was afraid something was wrong, and, being impatient to find out, started, myself. I thought Robinson & I reached the door at the same time. I did not see who opened it— It was he. I saw that two men came in, side by side. I was close by the door, & the one nearest me, was Fred. The side of his face was covered with blood, the rest very pale, his eyes full of intense expression. I spoke to ask him what was the matter,—he could not answer me. On his right hand was the assassin. I do not remember how his face looked, his arms were both stretched out, he seemed rushing toward the bed. In the hand nearest me was a pistol, in the right hand a knife. I ran beside him to the bed imploring him to stop. I must have said "Don't kill him," for father wakened, he says, hearing me speak the word kill, & seeing first me, speaking to some one whom he did not see—then raised himself & had one glimpse of the assassin's face bending over, next felt the blows—and by their force (he being on the edge of the bed, where fear of hurting his broken arm, had caused him to lie for some time) was thrown to the floor. I cannot remember seeing him—nor seeing Payne—go around the bed—but Anna was in the room and saw it. I have no remembrance of going around the foot of the bed, to the other side, but I remember standing there, by the corner at the foot, & thinking "This must be a fearful dream!" Then I looked about and saw, first, what I had seen before I think, but more fully now—three men struggling beside the bed. I knew who they all were then. I could not tell the next day. But they were Fred & Robinson & the assassin—next I saw all the familiar objects in the room, the bureau, the little stand, the book I had been reading, all looked natural. Then I knew it was not a dream. I remember pacing the room back & forth from end to end—screaming. My screams wakened Gus. but I do not remember seeing him when he came in— then Payne & the others were [blank in Ms.] After a little time, it seemed to me—though all that had taken place must have been almost in an instant, some vague idea of calling for assistance carried me into the hall. I think that at that time the assassin & those struggling with him were by the door in Father's room, & that I passed them as I went out. I have a very indistinct recollection of the next moment, when I seemed to meet Mother on one side, and Anna on the other, both saying "What is the matter," and I said something about the man, (Payne) who came out struggling with some one, I afterwards learned it was Augustus. I

Lewis Payne, his head covered by a padded mask to prevent an attempt at suicide, awaits trial at the Penitentiary Building in the Washington Arsenal. The trial began May 9; on July 7, convicted by a military court, Payne was hanged. So were Mrs. Mary E. Surratt, who had run the boarding-house at which the conspirators met; George Atzerodt, who had been designated to murder Vice President Johnson; and David Herold, "the infatuated associate of Booth."

Leslie's Illustrated, MAY 27, 1865

think I saw the assassin stab Hansell,[13] as he, the assassin rushed headlong down the stairs. I do not know just when—but I remember in the hall with Mother and Anna asking me what happended, my saying "Is *that man* gone," and they said "what man." The first recollection I have of seeing Augustus—except when the assassin broke away from him, was with his forehead covered with blood. It seemed to me that every man I met had blood on his face. It seems to me that I saw Fred then. I did not open any window and cry "murder" as the report of Robinson's statement said, neither did I leave the room as then mentioned, but at the time I have stated.

I remember running back, crying out, "Where's Father?," seeing the empty bed. At the side I found what I thought was a pile of bed clothes—then I knew that it was Father. As I stood my feet slipped in a great pool of blood. Father looked so gastly I was sure he was dead, he was white & very thin with the blood

13 Emerick Hansell, messenger for the State Department.

that had drained from the gashes about his face & throat. Fred was in the room till after Father was placed on the bed. Margaret [14] says she heard me scream "O my God! Father's dead." I remember that Robinson came instantly, & lifting him, said his heart still beat—& he, with or without aid, laid him on the bed. Notwithstanding his own injuries Robinson stood faithfully at Father's side, on the right hand— I did not know what should be done. Robinson told me everything—about staunching the blood with cloths & water. He applied them on the right side, & I, kneeling on the bed, on the left, put them on a wound on that side of the neck. Father seemed to me almost dead, but he spoke to me, telling me to have the doors closed, & send for surgeons, & to ask to have a guard placed around the house. William had gone for Dr Verdi, & he came & had ice applied to the wounds. I ran down to the butlers pantry for ice. & saw a great many persons gathered about the door. While Dr V. was on Father's right side, & I engaged as before, the doctor who was himself greatly excited kept saying to me—(I was talking & making some exclaimations I believe) "Don't get excited, don't get excited— Then Father showed his conciousness by putting out his hand towards me in a soothing way, as if to bid me be calm, & reassure me. It seemed a great while to us before the doctors came, though they probably hastened on the earliest information of what had occured. William, the colored boy, having been accustomed to go for Dr Verdi on former occasions, went for him the first thing, so he was here sooner. The Tayloes were passing—M^r & Mrs T. & came in—& stayed I think all night— Mrs Tayloe was in the hall or some other room, & Mr T. in Father's room. The Surgeon General came, & stood by Father on the right, & Dr Norris came next & kneeling down to examinine the wounds said something like "Assassination in the vilest form—" A clot of blood upon father's chest, which I had taken for a stab, was found to be only blood that had collected there outside. We were assured that no artery was severed, & the wounds were not fatal. The little entry outside fathers door, & the stairway beyond, were thronged with inquiring men of every description— M. C.s—policemen, members of the press—etc— Everyone was asking us to tell more than we knew ourselves. Anna, at Fred's door resisted their entrance with great firmness, & I was unwilling to have any one come into father's room—for I could not reason calmly, & suspected everyone. At first Mother had supposed that the whole occurrence consisted in Father's being more than usually delerious, & that in that condition he had injured Fred. She had an indistinct view of

14 One of the Sewards' maids.

Gus and Payne struggling at the door, & supposed it to be father with a knife. She saw Fred's condition & went into his room, & was engaged with him. He was then unable to speak. So she was not in father's room at first. I cannot remember when she came in—but I remember her being there, ministering to him. She & Anna went to the attic to see if any one was concealed there. Mother forbade me to go then— At one time I went, & searched in some of the rooms there, then went down to the parlor floor, & looked through three rooms & was going further when Fosburg told me he had searched. (Fosburg waited up stairs till Payne was out of the house—then appeared & stood at the foot of father's bed.) I remember going to the attic & tearing the clothing from the beds & bringing it down for father's bed when he had a severe chill. While the Surgeon General was here, I found between the door & the bed, just in front of the wash-stand, a hat which I supposed to be Payne's—as it afterwards proved to be— I showed it to Anna, & by her advice put it in the bureau drawer. The washbowl on the stand had the bottom broken out when I first looked at it. Near where I found the hat, the pistol was picked up— I found Robinson looking for the priming on the floor —he said it was missing, and if stepped on might do mischief—he soon found it. Dr Norris sewed up the great gash in father's cheek—which had laid open— I was standing by the door, against the wall while he did it. I imagined all the time that father suffered dreadfully. I thought I heard him moan. But Father has since told us that he remembers no feeling of pain, & that he thinks he both fell asleep & woke during the operation—he remembered "being sewed up." The Surgeon General was sent for with the news of the assassination of the President. Mother saw the person who came for him, who told her of the fact. I remember hearing some one else tell her the President had been shot. The Surgeon General sent me out of the room part of the time while they were attending to Father, & told me he would send for me if I was wanted. Perhaps it was at this time, I went into Fred's room & saw him lying bloody & unconcious, on a lounge, where he was being attended to. . . . I went across the hall into my own room. I was there twice. The first time they were dressing poor Hansell's back—(he was stabbed in the back) the second time he lay on the bed. Eliza the seamstress was there to attend to him. In the middle of the room sat Donaldson, his face buried in his hands—crying aloud, like a child. I touched his shoulder & said—"Donaldson, you were not hurt?" "No Miss Fanny" he said—"I wasn't here. If I had been here this wouldn't have happened. If I had been here I'd have been a dead man. Oh! why wasn't I here?"

All the white wood work of the entry was covered with great dashes of blood. I did not want it washed off—but Margaret & Eliza told me some person had directed that it should be—so I did not interfere. It was a terrible sight—there was so much blood everywhere. The drugget on the stairs was sprinkled with it, all the way down to the floor below. On the inner side of the door of Father's room there was, in blood, the distinct impression of a hand, which seemed to have clenched it from without. While this was being wiped off I marked the door, to show where the place had been. When we found father there was such a pool of blood that our dresses were drabbled in it. Dr Norris's assistant, Dr Nottson [15] came. Dr Norris bandaged Fred's wounds—which he supposed much less dangerous than they proved to be. The Surgeon General, having been summoned, went away. Father had been attended to & moved to the left side of the bed. As the Surgeon General left the room he shook hands with me telling me Father was safe. Dr Verdi at first for some time kept rushing around saying "Children, children, don't get excited—" While Father was being attended to, some of the time I stood over by the door, leaning against the wall. I think he came & said something of that sort once then. While I stood there Dr Norris came to me & said "You have been a pretty brave little girl tonight, can't you get me a shirt for your father?" & I went to get one of Augustus' who left his bed, & gave me two shirts. . . .

At one time all the doctors were in Fred's room, & Mother & I were with Father. Once I thought his wounds were bleeding afresh—but it proved to be only a clot of blood. At another time when the doctors were in the room, mother was sitting down—& I went to her. She was ill in some way I think—perhaps with palpitation. She showed feeling & anxiety that must have been anguish, but she bore up with the greatest fortitude—as we spoke together she told me she was afraid Fred could not live. By that time it had been ascertained that his injuries were very serious. I do not know whether it was before or after the Surgeon General left that Dr Wilson went to see Fred— He declined, on medical etiquette to examine the wounds till Dr Norris had removed the bandages put on by himself. It was found that Fred's injuries were of the most dangerous nature—the skull fractured. I met Mr Harrington in the entry—& he told me not to give up about Fred, described very serious injuries he had once sustained—had been trepanned. Fred was insensible. Father was conscious. Not very long after the attack, when Father's wounds had been dressed & himself moved to the right side of the bed, a number of distin-

guished gentlemen came in & stood about the bed. Mr Stanton, Gen. Halleck,[16] & Mr Welles [17] are all I remember. It was then that I first heard about the President, one of the gentlemen telling Mother that he was shot. As this group stood there Father related in a clear, distinct manner, his recollections of the whole scene—between each and he drew breath, as one dying might speak, & I feared the effort might cost his remaining strength. I think we gave him tea in the night —at his own request. I was in constant apprehension of some fatal turn in his symptoms— At length all was still in the room— We took our seats to watch through the night. Dr Norris remained much of the night—& when he went away left his assistant, Dr Nottson, saying that he was an accomplished physician. As we sat through those long dark hours the thoughts they brought were almost overwhelming. The thought that such cruel & inhuman beings, as the man who had attacked my father & brothers, existed, made me wish myself dead, & out of such a world anywhere seemed better. The anxiety of the condition of father & Fred was fearful. Although a guard sat in the entry, I could not reason away a feeling that the assassin who had wounded so many might return & finish his attempt. I had felt suspicious of every unknown face however friendly— I was too shocked to reason. "I have supped full on horrors," rang over & over in my mind—and I retraced the dreadful scene—& remembered the moment when I felt almost beside myself, and Anna's hand laid on my arm, & her voice "Fanny! Fanny!" recalled me, & I stopped screaming to answer her inquiries & to remember that I must be quiet & calm. Blood, blood, my thoughts seemed drenched in it—I seemed to breathe its sickening odor. My dress was stained with it—Mother's was drabbled with it—it was on everything. The bed had been covered with blood— the blankets & sheet chopped with several blows of the knife. Night wore away while we sat there—the gray light of morning came— "Risest thou then gray dawn again" repeated itself over & over in my mind—& that light should come, & the sun rise, & the birds sing & the green leaves rustle in the trees, seemed strange in such a world. Early in the morning, by Father's side, Dr Nottson showed me a card on which some one told one of the surgeons that the president was growing worse. Father asked about it. In the morning came a note from Miss Dix [18] to Mother, which I answered, offering to be of assistance, & to send one or more women nurses. Mr Stanton came. I think it must have been he—but perhaps it was some one earlier, that

[15] Brevet Major William Monroe Notson, Assistant Surgeon, U.S. Medical Corps.

[16] Major General Henry Wager Halleck, military advisor to the President and Chief of Staff of the Army.
[17] Secretary of the Navy Gideon Welles.
[18] Dorothea Lynde Dix, pioneer in the field of woman's nursing.

answered Mother's inquiry as to whether any thing later had been heard from the President— "Yes— He is dead." He died at 7—& we heard of it within two hours. While Mr Stanton was there by the bed Mother said very gently to Father— "Henry—the President is gone." He received the news calmly, but seemed to know the meaning of the words. He was not able to talk much of the time—and communicated, as he had done before the last injury—by means of a white slate & pencil—but—owing to his exhausted state, & to his broken arm, it was almost impossible for him to write so that it could be read. I remember that Mother said —in talking with the Secretary of War, "Are *you* safe Mr Stanton," as if apprehensive of danger to him— "Not any more than any one else" (or, the others,) he replied. He said Mrs Stanton was down stairs— I went down and saw her in the library— Mr Stanton came down, and I told him about the pistol—which was brought— I also told him of the hat & showed it to him—he took charge of both. I told him my fear about the guard, there not being any at the back door. He was very kind—& relieved my solicitude at once. a little Later in the morning I was called down to see Col. Pelouze, who said he had Mr Stanton's instructions to come to me, & to place the guard where I said. The guard was doubled—by Mr S.'s order, after my speak-

ing to him. Many friends came to inquire— I saw none of them but Dept. people. The President died about half past seven in the morning. Miss Dix sent a note which I answered—(she offered assistance) quite early she came over—& saw Mother & Father. Father conversed with her by using his slate. It was very difficult to read the writing—he was so weak. The following sentence, addressed to Miss Dix—I copied from the slate for her. "Neither the friends nor the enemies of our America have left me anything to complain of. The friends of America ought to have watched Mr Lincoln better. His life however is the forfeit. The Nation will do him Justice."

I copied three other sentences which he wrote on the slate that day—these: "—— the blows inflicted before or after the assault on you, Augustus, & Frederick," "I was fast asleep and only saw Fanny —— up, and the assasin. I next —— —— and would kill me. Then the blow, dashing blood in floods." (I have to leave blanks where the words were illegible.) "I saw all my strength was weakness last night. I thought that if I had still reserved forces I should make them take me safely through in two or three days.

I am very moderate.

I have drunk tea all day—making no point of it."

(Here this section of the diary ends.)

CHILDREN'S LITERATURE—PAST.

This is the Good Boy in the Old-Fashioned Story-Book.

CHILDREN'S LITERATURE—PRESENT.

This is "Billy the Biter; or, The Boy Butcher"—[See the Current Number of the *Boys' Own Hair-Raiser*.]

DOWN WITH COMIC BOOKS!

Parents should know what their children are reading. It will be news to many parents in Santa Fe that considerable literature of the blood and thunder kind is being read in this city. This is undoubtedly true in every other town of the territory. There is plenty of good literature interesting to children published nowadays at low prices, and there can be no excuse for children being allowed to read dime novels and wild, woolly west stories. The trouble lies in the home training and the scarcity of standard and periodical literature in many homes. A boy who has Cooper's and Scott's novels, Robinson Crusoe, a good juvenile magazine and his local daily paper to read at home will not go out and filch money to buy himself a blood and thunder story. A girl who has access to the standard novels of the day, to several volumes of fairly (*sic*) tales, to a good woman's journal and the daily paper will not pine for the Saturday Evening Gazette or the Family Story Paper with their perverse and silly love stories. Give children good literature to choose from, and their minds will stand in no danger of being poisoned by the flashy literature which finds too great a circulation in an enlightened country like the United States.

From the Santa Fe New Mexican, *April 7, 1900, reprinted in* Santa Fe, *by Oliver La Farge. Copyright 1959 by the University of Oklahoma Press.*

The Ultimate Courage of Jean de Brébeuf

CONTINUED FROM PAGE 59

Indians wagered literally everything—even their wives.

Very early in his missionary career de Brébeuf came to the conclusion that he would succeed in reaching these primitive people only if he shared their daily existence in every particular short of sin. And so, instead of building themselves a separate habitation, he and de Noüe accepted the openhanded hospitality of the native cabins.

It was a decision they would be forced to modify later on, if only to be able to observe their vow of chastity. For among the Hurons, men and women enjoyed complete sexual freedom both before and after marriage. Girls openly prostituted themselves as soon as they were old enough to do so. As a warning to later missionaries de Brébeuf wrote:

In France the great multitude and the good example of Christians, the solemnity of the Feasts, the majesty of the Churches so magnificently adorned, preach piety to you . . . in a word, you are almost beyond the danger of falling. . . . Here we have nothing, it seems, which incites toward good; we are among people who are astonished when you speak to them of God . . . Especially I would not dare to speak of the danger there is of ruining oneself among their impurities, in the case of anyone whose heart is not sufficiently full of God to firmly resist this poison.

It was a "poison" which, he sensed, would be a greater obstacle to their conversion than almost any other. Wisely, he decided not to launch a frontal attack upon it at once. There were other tasks, the most essential being to remove the barrier to communication.

Adept as he was at languages, de Brébeuf found that of the Hurons unusually difficult. Most of their words were made up of vowels, and they had no labial letters. The closest they could come to "Jean," in their guttural pronunciation, was "Echon," and this became at once their name for him. He also noted that "a relative noun with them always includes the meaning of one of the three persons of the possessive pronoun." Hence, when later in his mission he tried to teach them the Sign of the Cross he realized that they couldn't say, "In the name of *the* Father, and of *the* Son, and of *the* Holy Ghost." He wrote anxiously to his superior in Quebec asking if he might substitute: "In the name of *our* Father, and of *His* Son, and of *their* Holy Ghost."

It was a humbling task, for men so well educated, to begin learning new terms for the simplest objects and ideas. "Instead of being a great master and great Theologian as in France," de Brébeuf wrote, "you must reckon on being here a humble Scholar, and then, good

God! with what masters!—women, little children, and all the Savages,—and exposed to their laughter."

De Noüe, after a year of effort, had made almost no progress with the language, and this, combined with the fact that he did not possess de Brébeuf's facility for getting along with the savages, led him to return to Quebec in the summer of 1627. De Brébeuf and the Récollet de la Roche Daillon—who had come back from the western and southern tribes reporting a discouraging lack of progress—labored on through that summer, fall, and winter. Late the following June, the Récollet, too, returned to Quebec to rest and to report to his superior, leaving Jean de Brébeuf the only priest in Huronia. He would have faced the future with considerably less confidence had he known that an English fleet was approaching the St. Lawrence and that only by a bald-faced bluff would Champlain be able to stave off disaster.

Meanwhile, although in two years he had made not a single convert, de Brébeuf kept at his appointed task. As the leaves fell and biting cold ushered in the winter of 1628–29, his third among the Hurons, he set himself to studying the religious beliefs of the savages. He discovered that they did not have a clear concept of a creator but they did believe that the human soul was immortal, and that after the Feast of the Dead, which was held every ten or twelve years, the souls of all who had died since the last feast would proceed via the Milky Way, which the Hurons called "the path of souls," to a kind of heaven. The Hurons also believed there were good and bad spirits, both called *oki*, and that all the phenomena of Indian life—journeys and trading, wars and feasts, the flowing of streams and the blowing of the wind—fell under their jurisdiction. The Hurons sometimes made the bad *oki* offerings of tobacco; but they never prayed. As Francis Parkman said: "No race, perhaps, ever offered greater difficulties to those laboring for its improvement. . . . The primitive Indian, yielding his untutored homage to One All-pervading and Omnipotent Spirit, is a dream of poets, rhetoricians, and sentimentalists." De Brébeuf realized that to replace this mélange of legend and superstition with Christian concepts, many of which it was impossible even to express in the Huron language, would be a long process demanding almost superhuman patience.

He had hardly begun to confront his task when news of the previous year's unsuccessful attack on Quebec reached him in May of 1629. His superior,

102

fearful that the English would make another attempt soon, ordered him back to Quebec. He was bidden also to bring corn with him, for the enemy had blockaded the river and in the absence of supplies from France the tiny town was near starvation. Lescarbot's warning still went unheeded. By contrast, the English settlements to the south, founded at about the same time Champlain had landed at Quebec, were becoming more populous and increasingly self-sufficient. The French never closed the gap. In the end the failure would cost them a continent.

Five years passed before Jean de Brébeuf was able to return to Huronia, for the expected assault on Quebec—by a ridiculously small squadron of three ships under David, Louis, and Thomas Kirke, French Huguenots serving under the English—forced Champlain to strike his flag in July, 1629. The French governor, and the Jesuits with him, were carried to England by their captors, only to learn that the war between Britain and France had been concluded almost three months before the capture of Quebec. Under the terms of the ensuing treaty the French prisoners were to be released and Canada restored to its former masters. Negotiations dragged on until 1632, and two more years elapsed before de Brébeuf found himself once more in a Huron canoe, battling the current of the Ottawa on the way to the Freshwater Sea.

This time—and until its conclusion—the Huron mission was entirely Jesuit in character, for Cardinal Richelieu had decreed that only one religious order would be permitted to send missionaries to Quebec, and he had chosen the Jesuits over the Récollets. De Brébeuf, appointed superior in Huronia, was well-companioned; he had two other Jesuits, Fathers Ambroise Davost and Antoine Daniel, and six French laymen to help him. Arrived in Huronia, they persuaded the Indians to build them a house of their own, with a chapel at one end, a storage place at the other, and living quarters furnished in the Huron fashion in the center.

The house of the Frenchmen soon became a mecca for the savages, for at mealtimes, following the hospitable custom of the tribe, their kettle always contained enough *sagamité* to feed an extra guest. Moreover, rumor quickly spread through all the native cabins that the home of the "Blackrobes" and their companions was full of marvels. The few gadgets they had managed to bring with them—a prism, a magnet, a magnifying glass—were unremarkable in France, but to the Hurons they were a source of great wonder, and they opened a small wedge for the word of God.

For the first year or so they baptized almost no adults, partly because Daniel and Davost were still

Huron women wore loose-fitting clothing, an early Jesuit visitor noted, unlike contemporary Frenchwomen, who "try to have dresses fit as close as possible to the figure."

struggling with the language, partly because all three priests were wary of accepting insufficiently instructed converts whose backsliding would embarrass them later on. They did, however, baptize dying infants, and were in the Huron houses very often, succoring the sick from their tiny stock of medicines. Almost at once they set up an informal religious school for the children. One of the priests would chant the Our Father in Latin, another translating it into simple Huron rhymes as he went along. The Jesuits then taught their small charges a few Christian prayers, gave them a bit of catechetical instruction, and at dismissal rewarded their patience with trinkets or sweets. The missionaries thought they detected, among the children, some signs of progress, but the elders of the tribe rebuffed them, saying, "It is good for the French, but we are another people, with different customs."

With this kind of passive resistance the Jesuits felt they could cope; it was, after all, a matter of persistence, of finding a more effective approach. What they found harder was the open hostility of the Huron medicine men. The Hurons believed, with almost fanatic intensity, in the power of dreams, and the medicine men held sway over the people by professing to be able to interpret them. They also claimed they could cure—with weird incantations, incessant shell-rattling, and a bag of mysterious drugs—any illness to which a savage might fall victim.

Sometimes these ceremonial cures took the most outlandish and degrading forms. In one of them, called the Andacwandet, girls of the tribe would assemble around the sick person's pallet, and each would be asked which brave she would like to sleep with the following night. The chosen young men would come, and the couples would spend the night together in the patient's presence, while at each end of the lodge a medicine man sat chanting and rattling his shells. Moreover, the medicine men were adept at placing the blame for natural disasters—a crop failure, a prolonged drought, an epidemic—on the malevolent influence of the priests, so that not only the continuance of their mission but even their very lives sometimes hung by a very slender thread. Nevertheless, by 1636, de Brébeuf felt that the outlook for the Huron mission was brightening. Counting the period before the fall of Quebec, Jesuits had been in the Huron country for over five years. They were beginning to master the language, and in September three more priests, among them the redoubtable Isaac Jogues, arrived to double their numbers. The Hurons had begun to listen, at least, to what the priests told them of God and Heaven, and when one of them was in danger of death his relatives would request that he be baptized.

By early winter, de Brébeuf judged that the time for a frontal attack on the immorality of Huron life should be postponed no longer. A severe influenza epidemic was ravaging Huronia, and when the chiefs asked him to intercede for them with God, he decided to be blunt. "Do you wish to serve this Great Spirit," he asked, "and save yourselves from the pestilence that afflicts you?" When they answered in the affirmative he spoke without mincing words:

First, you must give up your belief in the power of dreams. Secondly, when you marry, you must bind yourselves to one woman for life; you must not change wives, you must not go to other women. Thirdly, you must not indulge in vomiting feasts, since God forbids such gluttony. Fourthly, you must not hold the Andacwandet, because such mating feasts offend God. Fifthly, you must not eat human flesh, even though it be that of your enemies. . . .

One of the chiefs replied (the translation is modern):

Echon, my brother, I must speak to you very frankly: I believe that your proposition is impossible. I cannot be a hypocrite. I express my thoughts honestly. I judge that what you propose will be a stumbling block. We have our own ways of doing things, you have yours and other nations have theirs. When you speak to us about obeying and acknowledging Him as our master, Who, you say, has made heaven and earth, you are talking of turning the country upside down. . . .

And the country, de Brébeuf concluded sorrowfully, was not yet ready to be turned upside down.

At least not by the Christian Gospel. Other forces were conspiring, however, to humble the Hurons. In 1635 a severe drought had swept the country, turning the green cornstalks to dried sticks in the fields. Intermittently over the next two years had come the influenza epidemic. Then, in 1639, there descended the worst scourge of all—smallpox—which killed the Hurons by the thousands and permanently pock-marked all who survived. As late as 1636 the Jesuits had estimated the population of Huronia at 30,000. A census which they conducted during 1639 and 1640 revealed that there remained no more than 12,000 souls.

Part of this alarming decimation was the result of the Hurons' continuing war of attrition with the Iroquois. To add to the Hurons' troubles, these fierce and bloodthirsty tribes, armed with muskets by the Dutch at Albany, began ranging far to the north and west from their villages in what is now central New York State.

For years the Iroquois had been sending into the Huron country small raiding parties which, in the words of one Jesuit, would "approach like foxes, fight like lions, and fly away like birds." The Hurons had reciprocated. Now, however, the Iroquois were out in force, and the toll they took was frightening.

It is probably not fair to the Jesuits to assume, as some historians do, that the wave of Huron conversions which they now began to experience was due entirely to the Indians' belief that by worshiping the Christian God they would obtain relief from the ravages of disease and at the same time cement their ties with the French, who in turn would save them from the Iroquois. For the Jesuits had greatly augmented their forces in Huronia—by 1639 there were thirteen priests—and they had continued to work selflessly, tirelessly, and with deepening insight.

In addition, they had recently changed their approach. On the bank of the River Wye they had decided to build a central mission station, a combined fort and residence, from which they would go out to the surrounding Huron towns. The station, which they called Sainte Marie, would serve not only as a spiritual headquarters for the priests, but as a rallying point where their Indian converts would be safe from the pagan influences of their villages. When in 1644 de Brébeuf returned from Quebec, where he had been sent to rest and to recover his strength after a bad fall on the winter's ice, he found Sainte Marie a thriving center manned by fourteen priests, two lay brothers, eleven *donnés* (laymen who had dedicated their lives

The chaousarou, *an armored, pike-like fish of Huronia.*

to the missions), and nine French workmen. These intensified efforts bore results. In the year 1646–47 alone, a total of thirteen hundred Indians asked for baptism. By contrast, six years before there had been only sixty Christians in all Huronia.

Yet there is little doubt that fear played its part in inducing the savages to rally around the cross. When in 1648 one of the pagan Hurons—who blamed the French for the peril in which the tribe now found itself—murdered a *donné*, the Huron chief apologized to the Jesuits in words eloquent of his people's condition:

My brother, I speak in the name of all eight Ouendat nations here assembled. We are now but a handful of people; you alone support this country. We are here to weep for your loss and ours. This country is now but a dried skeleton, without flesh, without veins, without sinews, without arteries. We are like dry bones tied together with threads. That wretched murderer thought he was aiming at the head of a young Frenchman. But he struck his own country and inflicted on it a deathly wound. My brother, have pity on this country.

Soon afterward the chiefs, among whom Christians now outnumbered pagans, declared Catholicism the official religion of the Huron tribes.

For the Jesuits, who had labored so long with such meager success, the victory was sweet. Yet it was tempered by a consciousness of impending tragedy. The Iroquois attacks were increasing in size and intensity, and the priests had already begun to suffer with their people. In 1646 Isaac Jogues and one of his *donnés*, Jean de La Lande, had been tortured and killed by the Iroquois. So, in 1648, had Antoine Daniel, de Brébeuf's companion for fourteen years. Any missionary who ventured out of Sainte Marie and remained in the Huron villages was taking his life in his hands.

Father de Brébeuf had not agreed with the idea of setting up a central mission-headquarters, believing that instead, priests should be stationed in each of the main Huron settlements. To him, separation meant alienation, and he had tried since the beginning of his ministry twenty years before to identify himself as closely as possible with his people. And so, although in obedience he joined his fellow Jesuits at Sainte Marie, he asked—and was granted—permission to spend most of his time serving five outlying villages.

It was in one of these, which the French called St. Louis, that he found himself on the morning of March 16, 1649, in the company of young Father Gabriel Lalemant, who had come to Huronia only six months before. The two priests had just finished saying their morning masses when out of the forest burst three Huron braves from a neighboring village, almost breathless, fear written on their faces. "The Iroquois!" they shouted. "We alone escaped!"

In despair, the villagers of St. Louis took up the cry. "The enemy! The Iroquois!" After an initial moment of shock, de Brébeuf and Lalemant thought about the aged, the women, and the children of St. Louis, who numbered perhaps four hundred. They must be evacuated. Quickly, adopting confident tones to stem the rising tide of panic, they hastened among the rude streets and into the lodges, gathering their flock and shepherding them along the trail toward safety. Finally, when only the able-bodied fighting men remained—they numbered less than one hundred—one of them, a Christian, shouted to the priests, "My brothers, save yourselves. Go now, while there is still time." But the Jesuits refused.

Suddenly the Iroquois were on them with a rush. As the defenders began falling, the two priests seemed to be everywhere at once, giving absolution to their converts and baptizing the unbelievers. Once the Iroquois were driven back. Again they came on with redoubled fury, and this time the fight was fierce but brief. In a few moments only about sixty Hurons were left alive, and these, finding themselves ringed about by hostile tomahawks and muskets, laid down their arms.

The captives were herded with sticks and clubs toward the nearby town of St. Ignace, the two Jesuits having been roughly stripped to the skin. At the entrance to the town all were forced to run a gantlet of screaming, mocking Iroquois, emerging on the other side bruised, slashed, and broken. About noon the torture began in earnest. De Brébeuf, whom the Iroquois evidently regarded as a special prize, was selected as the first victim, and Lalemant and the Hurons were made to witness his torments.

A simple recital of the separate cruelties they wreaked upon his giant frame makes it clear, without benefit of gruesome adjectives, that his torture has seldom been equaled in the whole Christian martyrology. First they tied him to a post and scorched his entire body with fire, seeking to silence him as he exhorted the Christians among the Hurons to keep up their courage and put their trust in God, who would welcome them into Paradise after the brief time of trial ahead. As he continued to speak, the Iroquois thrust burning brands down his throat, but still he cried out to his followers, *"Jésus taiteur!"* ("Jesus, have mercy upon us!") And from Lalemant and the Hurons the answer came back: *"Jésus taiteur!"* De Brébeuf had a moment of surcease as his torturers fashioned a rope of vines, strung metal axe-heads on it, and heated them red-hot in the fire. This they then placed around his neck. If he leaned forward, the axe-heads behind scorched his back; if he writhed backward, his chest felt the hot iron; if he stood still, the torture was doubled. As he bore each fresh torment without flinching or crying out, the fury of the Iroquois mounted. Next they fastened a girdle of pitch-filled bark around his waist and loins and set fire to it, but he still shouted encouragement to his flock. A renegade Huron who had been adopted into one of the Iroquois tribes now came close to de Brébeuf and said to him: "Echon, you have often told us that we must be baptized in order that we may have eternal happines after we die. In turn, we wish to be the cause of your happiness in heaven. Thank us, then, for the good turn we do you." And, carrying out kettles of scalding water, they poured them over his head in derision of the Sacrament. Still the beleaguered Jesuit cried out, "Jésus taiteur!" At last, in a frenzy, the Iroquois came at him in a group, hacking at his flesh with their knives until a chief finally cut out his heart and ate it in triumph, thinking to absorb some of the white man's prodigious courage. After four horrible hours Father Jean de Brébeuf, "the Ajax of the mission," was dead.

Though he was far less sturdy of body, Lalemant, whose trial began at nightfall, survived for fifteen hours, probably because the Indians revived him periodically through the long night so that they might save him for a dawn sacrifice to one of their gods. He endured as bravely as de Brébeuf and died with equal heroism, exhorting the Huron Christians to the last.

Three days later, the Iroquois having temporarily withdrawn, a small group of Frenchmen ventured cautiously out from Sainte Marie to see what had happened, and there, in the ashes of St. Ignace, they came upon "the relics of the love of God." Christophe Regnaut, a donné assigned to the search party, described what he saw in moving terms:

I examined first the Body of Father de Bréboeuf, which was pitiful to see, as well as that of Father L'alemant. Father de Bréboeuf had his legs, thighs and arms stripped of flesh to the very bones; I saw and touched a large number of great blisters . . . from the boiling water which these barbarians had poured over him in mockery of Holy Baptism. I saw and touched the wounds from a belt of bark, full of pitch and resin, which roasted his whole body. I saw and touched the marks of burns from the Collars of hatchets . . . I saw and touched his two lips, which they had cut off because he constantly spoke of God while they made him suffer. . . . In fine, I saw and touched all the wounds of his body . . . we buried these precious Relics on Sunday, the 21st day of March, 1649, with much Consolation. . . .

The Iroquois had done their work well. Within two weeks after de Brébeuf's death fifteen Huron villages had been abandoned, and the Hurons were finished as a nation. Most of the survivors fled through the forest and eventually sought adoption into other tribes. The remainder—a few hundred in number, mostly widows, children, and old men—huddled about the fortress of Sainte Marie. Against their better judgment the Jesuits allowed themselves to be persuaded to lead a migration to nearby Ahoendoe (now Christian) Island in Lake Huron, having first burned Sainte Marie, "the cradle of this Christian Church," to prevent its falling into enemy hands.

The move was a mistake. The food they had brought with them was soon gone, and the resources of the island were quickly exhausted. As winter approached, news came to them that several bands of Iroquois were encamped on the mainland to the south, waiting to exterminate any foraging party and cut off any escape in that direction. In their extremity the Hurons were reduced to eating, "in secret, and with horror," the bodies of their own dead.

In June of the next year, 1650, Father Ragueneau, the Jesuit superior, led about three hundred of the survivors northward in canoes through Lake Huron and down the Ottawa to the St. Lawrence, where the remainder joined them in the autumn. "It was not without tears," Ragueneau wrote, "that we quitted the country that owned our hearts and held our hopes, which had already been reddened by the glorious blood of our brethren, which promised us a like happiness, and which opened to us the road to heaven and the gate of paradise. Mais quoy! One must forget self, and relinquish God's interests for God's sake."

Thus ended the Huron mission, the most ambitious the Jesuits were ever to undertake in New France. It probably employed more priests (twenty-nine in all), it certainly produced more martyrs, and its loss was in a way the most crushing defeat the Canadian Jesuits ever suffered. When it ended there were still, it is true, some great days ahead for the Society in New France, as well as in parts of what would later become the United States. But the Blackrobes had identified themselves with the Hurons as with no other Indian nation, succoring them in adversity and even sharing their extinction. In the process they had sacrificed their own best men and expended their zeal's first bright flowering.

And yet, in their own minds, the price was not too high. Among the Hurons and other tribes, within a brief seven years, eight missionaries—de Brébeuf, Lalemant, Jogues, three other priests, and two donnés—achieved martyrdom and, eventually, sainthood. As Jean de Brébeuf had once written: "Jesus Christ is our true greatness; it is He alone and His cross that should be sought in running after these people, for, if you strive for anything else, you will find naught but bodily and spiritual affliction. But having found Jesus Christ in His Cross, you have found the roses in the thorns, sweetness in bitterness, all in nothing."

The Herald Angels of Woman's Rights

CONTINUED FROM PAGE 21

Phillips was there; so were Theodore Tilton and Mrs. Stanton. Phillips waxed warmly eloquent: now was the time to win the vote for the Negro, he urged, but the issue should not be clouded by simultaneously proposing the vote for women. Tilton nodded. Mrs. Stanton nodded. But Miss Anthony most emphatically did not nod. She would, she stated coldly, sooner cut off her right hand than ask for Negro suffrage and not woman suffrage. Whereupon she stalked out. "What does ail Susan?" asked Tilton plaintively. "I can not imagine," Mrs. Stanton answered; "I never before saw her so unreasonable and absolutely rude."

And so there was a little rift within the reformers' lute, but it did not make the music mute and slowly silence all. On the contrary, all voices were raised, and ever more loudly. Miss Anthony and Mrs. Stanton patched up their differences that same night. "Do tell me what is the matter with me," wailed Mrs. Stanton, as soon as Miss Anthony walked in upon her. "I feel as if I had been scourged from the crown of my head to the soles of my feet!" But the split between them and their quondam male allies grew wider. One of the most staunch, Horace Greeley of the New York *Tribune*, told them: "Your turn will come next. I conjure you to remember that this is the Negro's hour and your first duty now is to go through the State and plead his claims." And when the women objected, Greeley said bluntly: "If you persevere in your present plan, you need depend on no further help from me or the *Tribune*."

Nor did he support Mrs. Stanton when, quixotically claiming that while the law forbade women to vote it did not exclude them from office, she ran for Congress in 1866. (The voters of the Eighth New York District gave her twenty-four votes.)

Deliberately she and Miss Anthony widened the split still further. The following spring there was a state constitutional convention in New York, and Greeley was chairman of the committee on suffrage. It was their big chance to be politic. "Miss Anthony," said Greeley, "you know the bullet and the ballot go together. If you vote, are you ready to fight?" "Yes, Mr. Greeley," she answered, "just as you fought in the late war—at the point of a goose-quill." The unfortunate man was so ill-advised as to put his same question to Mrs. Stanton. "Yes, we are ready to fight, sir," Mrs. Stanton answered in her turn, "just as you did in the last war, by sending out substitutes." By now Greeley was mincemeat, but still they were not through with him. They knew he was preparing to file a committee

report against woman suffrage; they knew his chief argument would be that women did not really want the vote. And so, with exquisite timing, they caused to be presented a petition for woman suffrage on which the first name was that of Mrs. Horace Greeley. They had the satisfaction of hearing the audience in the committee room roar with laughter—but they had forever lost an ally.

Malice gratified is not worth friendship lost. Obduracy had stripped the ladies, one by one, of nearly all their influential comrades. Where now were they to turn? Back to Kansas, where the citizens had been given the opportunity, by referendum, to enfranchise women and Negroes. Lucy Stone was already stumping the state on behalf of women, and now Mrs. Stanton and Miss Anthony went west to join her. Their mission was fruitless (only nine thousand of some thirty thousand votes were cast for woman suffrage), but before they came home again they had found a new ally, surely the oddest ever recruited to their cause. His name was George Francis Train.

Train was rich, eccentric, and quite possibly the most self-satisfied human being of the entire nineteenth century. A jaunty, dapper man with a penchant for exotic toilet waters, Train had helped organize the Crédit Mobilier, the malodorous construction company that built the eastern half of the Union Pacific Railroad. He had withdrawn from this connection, however, in time to avoid being tarred by the scandals that would later blacken the company's name, choosing instead to concentrate on speculation in real estate along the railroad's right of way. By 1867 he was sufficiently wealthy to indulge in the care and feeding of

A satire on the aims of Mrs. Stanton and Miss Anthony was this cartoon of 1874 entitled "A Woman's Rights."

his whims, which were to range from supporting the Greenbackers to nominating himself for President of the United States.

The cause of woman's rights was made to order for Train. Three weeks before election day he appeared in Kansas, manic as a rubber ball, and took charge. On a platform he sparkled, spouting jokes to charm the electorate a dozen to the minute. Indeed, Miss Anthony's biographer, Katharine Anthony, credits to his efforts most of the nine thousand Kansas votes cast for woman suffrage. "Where is Wendell Phillips today?" Train demanded:

Where is William Lloyd Garrison? . . . Where is Henry Ward Beecher? . . . Where is Theodore Tilton? . . . Not one of [the] old army generals at hand; nobody but the rank and file of the Democratic party, and that wonderful, eccentric, independent, extraordinary genius and political reformer of America, who is sweeping off all the politicians before him like a hurricane, your modest, diffident, unassuming friend, the future President of America—George Francis Train!

An irresistible force; and so, when he asked Miss Anthony why she did not publish a journal, he swept away her obvious answer—that she had no money—and

CULVER SERVICE

calmly announced, "I will give you the money." She was staggered. He not only repeated his offer but invited her and Mrs. Stanton to join him ("Be my guests") on a month-long lecture tour from Omaha to New York.

For the newspaper he planned for them Train already had a name: *The Revolution;* and a slogan: "Men, their rights, and nothing more; women, their rights, and nothing less." He also had a staff in mind: proprietor, Susan B. Anthony; editors, Elizabeth Cady Stanton and Parker Pillsbury. How did it all seem to them? Like a dream compounded of hashish. They inhaled deeply.

But the dream came true. Less than a month after their return to New York, Train had opened offices for them on Park Row, Pillsbury had been hired away from the *Anti-Slavery Standard*, and the first issue of *The Revolution* was on the newsstands, datelined January 8, 1868. Their triumph, however, was freighted with woe. For their partnership with Train afforded their erstwhile allies a splendid excuse for rejecting them utterly. Garrison washed his hands of them, calling Train "that crack-brained harlequin and semi-

lunatic." And Wendell Phillips, approached by Mrs. Stanton at a reception in Boston, stonily folded his hands behind his back, withdrew a step, and refused to acknowledge her. Lucy Stone, too, denounced them, complaining of "the spectacle Miss Anthony is making of woman's cause by parading through the country with such a man as Train." Had the two suffragist heroines isolated themselves completely? So for a time it seemed.

Antagonisms boiled over at the woman's rights convention in 1869. Miss Anthony had labored above and beyond the call of duty to help make the convention a success. She had even gone to the office of Jay Gould and Jim Fisk to ask if they would not permit delegates to travel on the Erie Railroad at half fare. Here was an unlikely interview: the queen of the strong-minded females confronting Prince Erie himself, whose reputation for dalliance with fancy ladies was already a hissing and a byword, and would before long get him shot to death. What would a Jim Fisk think of a Susan B. Anthony? According to an account of her visit printed in *The Revolution,* she made her request of Gould and, while she was doing so, Fisk got up, came over, stared at her in silent wonder for fourteen long seconds, and then strode back to his desk. But she got her delegates to New York for half fare.

And for her trouble, she was greeted with a demand that she and Mrs. Stanton forthwith resign from the Equal Rights Association. This demand was, moreover, backed up by what appeared to be a majority. Faced with defeat, the two moved swiftly, and in the classic pattern of the American radical. Bearing a banner with the familiar device "Principle!" they galloped off at the head of a tiny splinter of the loyal and like-minded and, in a matter of hours, formed an entirely new organization, the National Woman Suffrage Association, of which Mrs. Stanton was of course the president. They were almost alone, but they were in complete command.

Have we here the stuff of heroines? Miss Anthony, for her part, was condemned on all sides. Ordinary folk rejected her because she was an unabashed and stubborn rebel. Radical folk rejected her because she was brusque, tactless, domineering, and incorrigibly cocksure—or, what was worse, hen-sure. As for Mrs. Stanton, her chief fault seemed to be that she would not dissociate herself from Miss Anthony; but in the circumstances that was enough. The list of charges against Miss Anthony grew steadily, leading Lucy Stone, Julia Ward Howe, and the other respectable suffragists to form their own group, the American Woman Suffrage Association. But what her critics within the suffrage movement found least excusable was her naïve acceptance of Victoria Woodhull.

Accompanied by her equally bewitching sister, Tennessee Claflin, Mrs. Woodhull had burst upon New York City in 1868 and, in a trice, had wangled an introduction to the richest man in the country, Commodore Cornelius Vanderbilt, and won his backing in an enterprise—Woodhull, Claflin & Co., Brokers—that stunned Wall Street numb. Victoria was just past thirty, "Tennie" was in her early twenties; no more alluring brokers ever operated. In three years they would gross seven hundred thousand dollars. More important, as soon as Victoria had begun to accumulate capital, she had preened herself and proclaimed her candidacy for President of the United States. In May, 1870, she published the first issue of a periodical unique in the annals of American journalism, *Woodhull & Claflin's Weekly*, in which she was to stump fearlessly for free love, short skirts, easier divorce laws, vegetarianism, world government, magnetic healing, birth control, abortion, abolition of the death penalty, an excess profits tax, legalized prostitution, public housing, and socialism. Such a greedy golloping of every highly spiced reform on the menu impressed the more unbalanced liberals of her time. When she appeared to survive the diet with no blatantly carminative effects, they made her welcome in their circles. Victoria, a willful woman, promptly ensnared some of the more susceptible males.

Henry Ward Beecher, for example, the eminent divine of Plymouth Church in Brooklyn, who had served briefly as president of the respectable American Woman Suffrage Association, was a susceptible male. Victoria had fixed her large brown eyes on Beecher warmly enough to make tongues wag.

For another example there was the journalist Theodore Tilton, a Beecher protégé who had served briefly as president of the radical National Woman Suffrage Association. As to his susceptibility there could be no doubt: he and Victoria had carried on a tempestuous affair for several months, during which they were constant, devoted companions.

Most of the women, however, were notably unsusceptible. When the question was put, "Who is Victoria? what is she, that all our swains commend her?" the women answered coldly, "She is a hussy," and as one they slammed their doors in the fair Victoria's face.

All but Miss Anthony. When she heard that Victoria was to deliver a memorial in favor of woman suffrage before the Judiciary Committee of the House of Representatives, Miss Anthony impulsively joined her before the committee and later invited her to a seat of honor on the platform at her society's national convention. This led to what was promptly called the Woodhull Convention by all the newspapers, the reporters joyfully asserting that the purpose of the meeting was not suffrage but free love. (The respectable suffragists, meeting in New York at the same time, sniffed audibly and passed a resolution condemning free love.)

Nor was Mrs. Stanton a model of discretion and political acumen during this period. In April, 1872, ensnared by Mrs. Woodhull's plausible wiles, she signed her own name as well as Miss Anthony's to a proposal to transform the National Woman Suffrage Association into a new People's party that would nominate candidates for the coming presidential election. When she got wind of this demented scheme, Miss Anthony exploded. She demanded that Mrs. Stanton retract; but her old partner merely called her meddlesome and autocratic, and went into retreat, refusing to stand again for president of the association. Faced with the task of protecting the cause of woman suffrage from Mrs. Woodhull, whom she had tardily recognized as perhaps a wee bit opportunistic, Miss Anthony showed how autocratic she could be.

When Mrs. Woodhull (with Mrs. Stanton's backing) asked if her People's party might share the Suffrage Association's convention hall, Miss Anthony refused. When Mrs. Woodhull showed up anyway and moved to have the suffragists join her People's party at *her* convention hall, Miss Anthony banged her gavel fiercely and, when a majority voted against her, declared the entire proceeding out of order and the association's convention adjourned. When Mrs. Woodhull nevertheless continued speaking, to the evident relish of most of those present, Miss Anthony summarily instructed the janitor to put out the lights. No Woodhull was going to capture *her* splinter.

Having routed Mrs. Woodhull, Miss Anthony had time to muse on a friend's folly: "Never did Mrs. Stanton do so foolish a thing," Miss Anthony told her diary; and again: "I never was so hurt with folly of Mrs. Stanton."

But Mrs. Stanton's folly was far greater than even Miss Anthony had reckoned. It is written, "As a jewel of gold in a swine's snout, so is a fair woman which is without discretion," and Mrs. Stanton was so indiscreet as to confide to Mrs. Woodhull the juiciest bit of scandalous gossip of the age. Mrs. Woodhull filed the gossip away for future reference; who knew when it might not come in handy? Just now, however, she had more urgent matters on her mind. In the campaign of 1872 her People's (now Equal Rights) party was not creating sufficient stir to suit her. The suffragists had not, as expected, forwarded her fortunes. Could she perhaps blackmail some of them? She tried, but to no avail. She then clamped her pretty lips together and lighted a slow-burning fuse. She would show them; she would show them all. She would print in her *Woodhull & Claflin's Weekly* the story she had heard from Mrs. Stanton.

On November 2, 1872, three days before election, *Woodhull & Claflin's Weekly* hit the streets with a long, vivid, detailed story so zippy that by evening, copies were changing hands at forty dollars apiece. This was the article that alleged adulterous physical intimacies between Henry Ward Beecher, the country's most renowned clergyman, and Elizabeth Tilton, wife of his close friend and associate, Theodore Tilton. Naturally it rocked the nation.

Had the adulteries actually taken place? The question was never satisfactorily answered, even by a jury impaneled for the purpose. At all events, Mrs. Tilton was convinced that the Seventh Commandment had been, if not broken, at least severely bent. She confessed her frailties first to her husband and then, obsessed with guilt, to a few of her friends. One night when Miss Anthony was her guest, Mrs. Tilton had climbed into Miss Anthony's bed and given her a full account. As it happened, Tilton had himself told the same story to Mrs. Stanton earlier that same day. When presently Miss Anthony fed it back to Mrs. Stanton, everything checked.

And still it might have stayed where it was, in the realm of gossip, except that Mrs. Stanton retailed it all to Victoria Woodhull. Did she do so deliberately, guessing what Mrs. Woodhull might do with it? It is not impossible; for Mrs. Stanton had never been fond of clergymen and their sturdily obstructive role where woman's rights were concerned. Nor had she ever forgiven Beecher for accepting the presidency of the respectable American Woman Suffrage Association.

In any case, as soon as the story was in print, various celebrated American eccentrics eagerly clamored to get into the act. Anthony Comstock, that zealous protector of the public morals, was the first to move: he had Mrs. Woodhull and her sister jailed for printing obscenity. And now here came George Francis Train again, all elbows, crying out that there was nothing obscene in what the sisters had published and, to prove his point, printing some carefully culled verses from the Old Testament that were, he insisted, far more obscene. He was jugged too—in, he later claimed, Cell Number 56 of the Tombs, just across the corridor from Edward S. Stokes, who had killed Jim Fisk over Josie Mansfield, and one cell removed from Richard Croker, who would before long be the Grand Sachem of Tammany Hall.

At the least, all this foofaraw distracted public attention from the campaign for woman suffrage, and **upstate in Rochester Miss Anthony had reason to be**

hot with rage. For on the day before the scandalous story had been printed, she had planned "a fine agitation"; at the head of a group of sixteen women, she had marched into the registration office of the Eighth Ward in Rochester and, invoking her rights under the Fourteenth Amendment, had demanded to be registered as a voter. All sixteen women had been duly registered; on election day all sixteen voted; and, sure enough, all sixteen were subsequently arrested. But their contumacy had not got the space in the papers for which Miss Anthony had hoped.

She came to trial in June, 1873. It was clear that the poor, timorous males were gravely affrighted by her gesture: a justice of the United States Supreme Court, Ward Hunt, was on hand to preside, and his sympathies were evident from the outset. Although it was a criminal case, Hunt directed the jury to find Miss Anthony guilty, refused permission to poll the jurors, and dismissed them before they could blink. A smooth, if highhanded, procedure, and marked by only one error. That was when Hunt inquired: "Has the prisoner anything to say why sentence should not be pronounced?"

But of course she had; a great many things; and she got in a solid five minutes' worth of agitprop while Hunt feebly protested, interrupted, tried to hush her up, gaveled, colored beet-red, and ordered her seated. He then fined her one hundred dollars and costs, to which she retorted that she would "never pay a dollar of your unjust penalty." Hunt was shrewd enough not to impose a prison term until the fine had been paid; if he had, she would have been able to appeal and win a reversal because she had been denied proper trial by jury.

And now a curious change came about. Perhaps it was because of the obvious unfairness of her trial, perhaps because of a belated recognition of her dogged persistence, perhaps only because she was now well along in her fifties—but imperceptibly her public image had mellowed. Respect crept into the editorial comment about her, displacing the derisive contempt. "No longer in the bloom of youth," said one St. Louis newspaper, "—if she ever had any bloom—hard-featured, guileless, cold as an icicle, fluent and philosophical, she wields today tenfold more influence than all the beautiful and brilliant female lecturers that ever flaunted upon the platform as preachers of social impossibilities."

Something of the same sort was happening to the public concept of her cause. It was no longer radical. It was a long, long way from being achieved but, having become familiar, it was now grown respectable. Miss Anthony and Mrs. Stanton both recognized it: they sat down together to write the history of their efforts, a tacit admission that the old war horses were beginning to think of oats in the stable. Miss Anthony found time for a trip to Europe; for the first time in her life she took her breakfast in bed. "A purposeless life," she wrote acidly, and bestirred herself to form yet another organization, the International Council of Women. Mrs. Stanton, too, had slowed down; Miss Anthony was obliged to harass her into attending annual conventions.

A new generation was coming along, dissatisfied with the meager results achieved by the old. For one thing, the youngsters demanded that the two suffrage associations combine; the overlapping of effort was silly. For another, they looked on Miss Anthony and Mrs. Stanton and Lucy Stone as embarrassing symbols of the past, best fitted for such ceremonial functions as the celebration of seventieth or eightieth birthdays, to serve the sweet purposes of publicity.

Mrs. Stanton was ready for such serenity, but not Miss Anthony. Still incorrigibly meddlesome, she resisted all efforts to nudge her into retirement, seeking to keep an iron grip on such procedural matters as the nomination and election of new officers. But it was manifest that her grip on the woman's rights movement was being prized open.

In 1899 Miss Anthony retired. She was eighty; but she had only banked her fires, there was still much to do—the history of her long fight to finish, her memoirs to write; and so much to think back on. What, after all, had she and Mrs. Stanton accomplished? Yes, they had created a climate of opinion, perhaps; but what of a specific, concrete nature? Where could women vote? Only in Wyoming, in Colorado, in Idaho, in Utah. To be sure, a few laws had been passed and a few customs altered: women could own their own property now, and could go to college; there was increasing agitation to control the evil of drink, and women were taking a leading part; all this was worth reflecting on. But women still had no vote.

In 1902 Mrs. Stanton died. Miss Anthony traveled from Rochester to New York for the funeral. "Oh, this awful hush!" she exclaimed, on entering the empty house. "It seems impossible that voice is stilled which I have loved to hear for fifty years . . . The papers, I believe, had good editorials—I have read them but I do not know, I can think of nothing . . ."

And still Miss Anthony persisted, a steady convention delegate, an indefatigable puller of strings, an untiring committeewoman. At eighty-four she traveled to Germany for a convention of the International Council of Women, hailed as the "grand old woman of America"; at eighty-five she journeyed across the continent for a suffragist convention in Oregon; at eighty-six, sick and very feeble, she appeared at her

last convention, in Baltimore. She was given a ten-minute ovation. But when she spoke she showed that her reflection had been bitter. "I have looked on many such audiences," she said, "and in my life time I have listened to many such speakers, all testifying to the righteousness, the justice, and the worthiness of the cause of woman suffrage . . . The fight must not cease; you must see that it does not stop."

CULVER SERVICE

At her birthday celebration a few days later a congratulatory telegram was handed her; it came from President Theodore Roosevelt. "When will men do something besides extend congratulations?" she cried. "I would rather have President Roosevelt say one word to Congress in favor of amending the Constitution to give women the suffrage than to praise me endlessly!" And once again the applause broke out.

Back home in Rochester she was put to bed. Anna Shaw came to visit early in March, 1906. She stayed a week. One day, when Dr. Shaw was sitting beside her bed, Miss Anthony held up her hand and measured a little space on one finger. "Just think of it," she whispered, "I have been striving for over sixty years for a little bit of justice no bigger than that, and yet I must die without obtaining it. Oh, it seems so cruel!" Two days later she was dead.

For each woman, Mrs. Stanton and Miss Anthony, a long, hard life; for each, more than eighty-six years; for each, more than a half-century of struggle and self-sacrifice, of insult and sneers and derision, of belated respect and honor; for each, death before her hopes could be realized. It is the common fate of the radical reformer. They have, of course, their lasting monument—the Nineteenth Amendment, granting suffrage to women. But Mrs. Stanton had, in a letter to Miss Anthony years before, written their joint and fitting epitaph. "Such pine knots as you and I," Mrs. Stanton wrote, "are no standard for judging ordinary women."

Peter Lyon, a free-lance writer living in New York City, has written for AMERICAN HERITAGE *on a number of other notable figures of the nineteenth century, among them Peter Cooper (February, 1959), Isaac Singer of sewing-machine fame (October, 1958), and George C. Tilyou, the impresario of Coney Island (June, 1958).*

A Slave's Memory of Mr. Jefferson

Mr Jefferson was a tall strait-bodied man as ever you see, right square-shouldered: nary man in this town walked so straight as my old master: neat a built man as ever was seen in Vaginny, I reckon or any place—a straight-up man: long face, high nose. . . .

Old master was never seen to come out before breakfast—about 8 o'clock. If it was warm weather he would'nt ride out till evening: studied upstars till bell ring for dinner. When writing he had a copyin machine: while he was a-writin he would'nt suffer nobody to come in his room: had a dumb-waiter: When he wanted anything he had nothing to do but turn a crank & the dumb-waiter would bring him water or fruit on a plate or anything he wanted. Old master had abundance of books: sometimes would have twenty of 'em down on the floor at once: read fust one, then tother. Isaac has often wondered how old master came to have such a mighty head: read so many of them books: & when they go to him to ax him anything, he go right straight to the book & tell you all about it. He talked French & Italian. . . .

Mr Jefferson had a clock in his kitchen at Monticello; never went into the kitchen except to wind up the clock. He never would have less than eight covers at dinner—if nobody at table but himself: had from eight to thirty two covers for dinner: plenty of wine, best old Antigua rum & cider: very fond of wine & water. Isaac never heard of his being disguised in drink. He kept three fiddles: played in the arternoons & sometimes arter supper. This was in his early time: When he begin to git so old he did'nt play: kept a spinnet made mostly in shape of a harpsichord: his daughter played on it. Mr Fauble a Frenchman that lived at Mr Walker's —a music-man used to come to Monticello & tune it. There was a forte piano & a guitar there: never seed anybody play on them but the French people. Isaac never could git acquainted with them: could hardly larn their names. Mr Jefferson always singing when ridin or walkin: hardly see him anywhar out doors but what he was a-singin: had a fine clear voice, sung minnits (minuets) & sich: fiddled in the parlor. Old master very kind to servants.

—From *Memoirs of a Monticello Slave: As Dictated to Charles Campbell in the 1840's by Isaac, one of Thomas Jefferson's Slaves*